CIVIL WAR IN
TENNESSEE

Civil War in Tennessee

MISSOURI

VIRGINIA

NORTH CAROLINA

GEORGIA

KENTUCKY

ALABAMA

MISSISSIPPI

ARKANSAS

TENNESSEE R.

MISSISSIPPI R.

CUMBERLAND R.

DUCK R.

Cairo

Paducah

Columbus

Island #10

Ft. Pillow

Memphis

Memphis Naval Battle

Ft. Henry

Ft. Donelson

Ft. Johnson

Shiloh

Corinth

Mill Springs

Cumberland Gap

Rogersville

Bristol

Blue Springs

Greenville

Knoxville

Gettysburg

Chattanooga

Chickamauga

Gallatin

Hartsville

Carthage

Nashville

La Vergne

Stones River

Murfreesboro

Franklin

Spring Hill

Columbia

Pulaski

CIVIL WAR IN
TENNESSEE

STEVE COTTRELL

Illustrated by Andy Thomas

PELICAN PUBLISHING COMPANY
Gretna 2001

*The word "Pelican" and the depiction of a pelican are
trademarks of Pelican Publishing Company, Inc., and are
registered in the U.S. Patent and Trademark Office.*

Library of Congress Cataloging-in-Publication Data

Cottrell, Steve.
    Civil War in Tennessee / Steve Cottrell ; illustrated by Andy Thomas.
        p. cm.
    Includes bibliographical references and index.
    ISBN 1-56554-824-8 (pbk. : alk. paper)
        1. Tennessee—History—Civil War, 1861-1865—Campaigns. 2. United
States—History—Civil War, 1861-1865—Campaigns. I. Title.

E470.4 .C68 2001

2001032742

Printed in the United States of America

Published by Pelican Publishing Company, Inc.
1000 Burmaster Street, Gretna, Louisiana 70053

Contents

Preface

To compile and describe all the countless Civil War actions in Tennessee would be a monumental task taking the better part of a lifetime. The purpose of this small volume is to provide a broad overview of the region's conflict, briefly describing the main battles as well as a sampling of the smaller actions. As in my previous books, this informal work has been worded in an easy-to-read style for the average person to learn and enjoy a little history.

Every effort has been made to be historically accurate and non-partisan. The fact that I have ancestors who fought on both sides in the war helps me to be fairly non-biased in my accounts. My father's side of the family tended to be Union sympathizers, and my mother's side tended to be Confederate sympathizers. However, the ancestor I would like to single out for a special tribute here is my great-great grandfather who served in Tennessee during the war. John P. Cottrell was a private in the Sixth Indiana Cavalry Regiment. His military record states that he took part in the East Tennessee Campaign and the Siege of Nashville. This book is dedicated to John and brave men like him on both sides whose service in Tennessee should not be forgotten.

CIVIL WAR IN TENNESSEE

CHAPTER 1

Storm Clouds Gather: 1861

Rugged Tennessee: wooded mountains with clear streams and rocky bluffs, rolling fields with rich soil and abundant wildlife. Long ago this beautiful region was the setting for a brutal conflict that America could never forget. It was springtime in 1861 when young men's hearts were full of fire, and their ladies tearfully bade them farewell as they marched off to war. It was a time when most people rarely traveled fifty miles from home, yet over the next four years, countless Tennessee farm boys would march hundreds of miles and see incredible sights, both grand and terrible. It was a time when most Tennesseans felt the same way about their state as most Americans today feel about the United States. It was a time of fear when the Federal government was mustering its military might to prevent Tennessee and other Southern states from forming their own separate nation, the Confederate States of America. Those fiery young men in the spring of `61 believed they were following a virtuous path of patriotism as they boldly marched off to meet their destiny in the most horrific tragedy America has ever endured.

Interestingly, Tennessee at first did not embrace the secessionist movement. On February 9, 1861, the day after the Confederacy had been formed in Montgomery, Alabama, the state held a referendum in which its citizens voted to decline even to consider the question of secession. However, after the surrender of Fort Sumter, President Abraham Lincoln called on the non-seceded states to furnish troops to force the Confederate states back into the Union. Most Tennesseans were appalled at the idea of the Federal government using military force against Southern states choosing to leave the Union. They, like many other Americans, felt the seceding states should be allowed to go in peace. Their governor, Isham G. Harris, telegraphed the U.S. secretary of war, "Your dispatch of the 15th inst., informing me that Tennessee is called upon for two regiments of militia for immediate service is received. Tennessee will not furnish a single man for coercion, but 50,000 if necessary for the defense of our rights and those of our southern brothers."

Another referendum was held on June 8 in which Tennessee's citizens voted two to one for action leading to withdrawal from the Union. Most of those who voted to remain in the Union resided in the eastern portion of the state. On June 17, the new national flag of the Confederacy, the "Stars and Bars," was hoisted over the state capitol at Nashville. By June 18, the Provisional Army of Tennessee could muster twenty-four regiments of infantry (normally, at full strength, a regiment had about a thousand men), enough mounted companies to form a cavalry regiment, and ten batteries of artillery (eight guns per battery). Three Tennessee regiments had already been sent to Virginia where the first major clash of the war was expected soon. On June 24, Governor Harris announced, "All connection with the Federal Union is now dissolved, the State now being an independent government, free from all obligations to or connection with the United States." In July, Tennessee formally joined the Confederate States of America. By now, all but three of its representatives in the Federal Congress had left Washington. One of those remaining was Tennessee senator (and former governor) Andrew Johnson.

Southern patriotic fervor in Tennessee was at a peak as the war began. Private Sam R. Watkins of the First Tennessee Infantry Regiment described what he saw as he and his comrades traveled east by railroad across the state on their way to the front in Virginia: "Leaving Nashville, we went bowling along twenty or thirty miles an hour, as fast as steam could carry us. At every town and station citizens and ladies were waving their handkerchiefs and hurrahing for Jeff Davis and the Southern Confederacy. Magnificent banquets were prepared for us all along the entire route. It was one magnificent festival from one end of the line to the other. At Chattanooga, Knoxville, Bristol, Farmville, Lynchburg, everywhere, the same demonstrations of joy and welcome greeted us. Ah, those were glorious times. . . ."

During the first year of the war, violence in Tennessee came mainly from guerrilla activity in the eastern part of the state. In early June of 1861, Unionists in East Tennessee became increasingly violent. "Lincolnites," as they were called, organized and drilled military companies, seized political control of several counties, attempted to obtain weapons and ammunition, and initiated contacts with the Union army in Kentucky. Many simply chose to flee across the border into Kentucky and actually join the Federal army there.

The first commander of the Confederate Department of East Tennessee, Brig. Gen. Felix K. Zollicoffer, arrived in Knoxville in late July. His orders from the Confederate secretary of war stated that his primary responsibility was to secure the rail lines in his department and block Northern attempts to smuggle arms into the region. His second was to break up the Unionist political and military organizations and, if necessary, aid civilian authorities in suppressing treason. However, Zollicoffer chose to tolerate the presence of Unionists as long as they did not engage in rebellious activities. He ordered his troops to treat all civilians with respect and attempted to minimize contact between military personnel and civilians by frequently confining soldiers to their camps.

"Ah, those were glorious times. . . ."

However, not all Lincolnites escaped reprisals. In August, the Confederate Congress passed the Alien Enemies Act and followed it up with the Sequestration Act. The Alien Enemies Act defined anyone refusing to recognize the authority of the Confederate government as an alien enemy. Such persons were given forty days either to swear allegiance to the Confederacy or leave the South. Those who refused to swear allegiance to the Confederacy but remained in Confederate territory were subject to arrest and expulsion. The Sequestration Act stated that the property of an alien enemy was subject to confiscation and sale at public auction. East Tennessee Confederates aggressively used these acts against their Union neighbors, and for the next couple of years, the county courts were full of sequestration cases; as a result, countless Unionists lost their homes and property. Sequestration actions created a legacy of bitterness that led to brutal retaliation when the Federal government finally gained control of the region later in the war. The Alien Enemies Act and Sequestration Act hurt many Lincolnites in East Tennessee, but they also confirmed Unionist fears about the tyranny of Confederate rule; their overall effect was to actually stiffen loyalist resistance in the region.

While militant Unionists in East Tennessee mobilized for action, the Lincoln administration and Federal commanders formulated plans for the invasion of that portion of the state. In late June, the Federals were organizing Union recruits from Tennessee across the border in Kentucky and training them for an intended military invasion of their home state. In September, the outspoken East Tennessee Unionist, Rev. William B. Carter, met with the Federal army's general officers in Kentucky to present a brash plan of action. He then traveled to Washington, D.C., and presented the same plan to President Abraham Lincoln, Secretary of War Simon Cameron, and Maj. Gen. George B. McClellan. Carter suggested that Unionists could assist a Federal invasion of East Tennessee by destroying nine key bridges on the railroads connecting East Tennessee with Georgia, Virginia, and Middle Tennessee. This partisan sabotage would cut East Tennessee off from swift Confederate reinforcements, while an accompanying mass uprising by Tennessee Unionists would occupy the few Confederate troops already present in the region. Under these conditions, Carter reasoned, Federal troops could easily take East Tennessee. Carter's plan was received favorably, and he left Washington with twenty-five hundred dollars to finance his operation and the mistaken belief that he had a firm commitment for a military invasion.

Carter slipped back into East Tennessee, accompanied by two Union officers, Captains William Cross and David Fry, also Tennesseans. The three formed several small groups of

Unionist volunteers. Carter assigned one or two bridges to each group. He then chose the night of November 8 to carry out his bold, covert operation. He believed it would coincide well with the Federal military invasion of East Tennessee. Although aware of vague, verbal threats in the past by Unionists against the railroads, Confederate authorities had no knowledge of Carter's well-kept secret and did not have the railroad bridges properly guarded on the night his men struck.

Carter's Union partisans succeeded in destroying five of the nine targeted bridges: the Hiwassee River bridge in Bradley County, the Lick Creek bridge near Greeneville, the Holston River bridge in Sullivan County, and two spans over Chickamauga Creek near Chattanooga. The four bridges that were not destroyed were saved by Confederate guards. Nevertheless, transportation on three different railroads was disrupted; the trains came to a halt on the East Tennessee and Virginia Railroad, the East Tennessee and Georgia Railroad, and the Western and Atlantic Railroad. Carter's men also destroyed telegraph lines, cutting communications at critical points.

News of the bridge burnings and rumors that a Federal army had marched into Tennessee from Kentucky sparked a mass revolt by the Unionists in East Tennessee. But in fact, the Federal military invasion did not take place. Brigadier General William T. Sherman, in charge of the Department of the Cumberland, had cancelled the operation on November 5. Tennessee Unionist senator Andrew Johnson had frantically plead for Sherman to proceed with the invasion and even threatened to lead the East Tennessee troops himself, but it was to no avail. Sherman feared that Kentucky itself might be invaded by Zollicoffer's army and wanted his troops to remain ready in Kentucky if such an incursion occurred. Nevertheless, rumors that Federal troops were marching into Tennessee emboldened Unionists who mustered paramilitary companies with hundreds of members in several East Tennessee counties. The Confederate post commander at Knoxville reported, "The whole country is now in a state of rebellion."

William Tecumseh Sherman

Within hours of the bridge burnings and reports of a Unionist uprising, Confederate reinforcements were heading for East Tennessee. Brigadier General William H. Carroll brought two regiments from Memphis, and four additional regiments came from Middle Tennessee and Georgia. The continued threat of a Federal army invasion forced Zollicoffer to hold most of his forces on the border, but he did send one regiment to strengthen the defenses at Knoxville. These forces moved quickly to crush the Unionist rebellion.

General Carroll placed Knoxville under martial law, took control of all access into and out of the town, and ordered his troops to conduct a house-to-house search for weapons. Movements into and out of Chattanooga were also restricted. Secessionist civilian volunteers aided regular Confederate troops in attacking and dispersing camps of Unionists in more than a dozen counties. They then spread out into the country-side, going from farm to farm, arresting men reported as bridge burners, or said to have been at a Unionist camp, and transporting them to Knoxville for trial. The ordeal became a terrifying "witch hunt," with anyone at risk of arrest for simply having been said to have voted against secession. Evidence indicates that a few suspects were even shot or hanged on the spot when arrested without benefit of a trial. Military tribunals at Greeneville and Knoxville conducted hasty trials of Unionist prisoners and convicted seven men of bridge burning. The sentences of three of them were commuted, but four were executed by hanging according to the instructions of the Confederate secretary of war. More than two hundred other Unionists, including state senators, representatives, and local officials accused of involvement in the uprising, were sent to military prisons in the Deep South.

A fiery night in Tennessee

General Zollicoffer, who had tried to be lenient toward Unionists, became bitter and vindictive after the uprising. East Tennessee Unionists entered a period of great suffering from Confederate repression. Yet resistance stayed alive. After November of 1861, Unionists operated in smaller bands and sought limited objectives, relying on guerrilla tactics to achieve their goals. Some Secessionists would respond likewise, giving rise to vicious guerrilla warfare that would plague the state for the remainder of the war. Union guerrilla or "bushwhacker" leaders, such as "Tinker Dave" Beatty, and Confederate bushwhacker leaders, such as Champ Ferguson, would become infamous for their ruthless brand of merciless warfare.

Even though the violent activities of the bridge burners and the Union uprising had brought limited amounts of destruction and death to Tennessee in 1861, it was a far cry from full-scale war. Thus, Tennessee survived the war's first year with minimal damage. Yet it braced itself for what the new year might bring. Its strategic position had already sealed its fate. The beautiful state was destined to be one of the bloodiest battlegrounds of the war.

With the wisdom of hindsight, some historians now believe that Tennessee was the true key to the Confederacy's survival. The "Volunteer State" was one of the South's major producers of foodstuffs. The Confederacy's greatest iron production region lay in the state between the Cumberland and Tennessee Rivers. The largest gunpowder mills in the entire South lay along the Cumberland River northwest of Nashville. Also Nashville was the leading war materials production center in the West. The great Southern city blocked the invasion path to the vitally important industrial centers of Chattanooga and Atlanta. Yet as the war began, the primary concern of the highest levels of the Confederate government was the defense of their new nation's capital, which had foolishly been relocated from the relatively safe and distant site of Montgomery, Alabama, primarily for political reasons. The new site at Richmond, Virginia, was, from a strategic viewpoint,

audacious; located at the extreme northeastern border of the Confederacy near the Federal capital itself, it was a nightmare to defend. If basic logic had prevailed in the Confederate government, the capital would have been left far down in the Deep South, and the defense of Tennessee would have been of greater concern to the politicians.

The Confederacy's top military commander in the West (including Tennessee), Gen. Albert Sidney Johnston, successfully bluffed Federal forces for nearly the entire first year of the war; the Yanks had no idea how weak Johnston's defensive line really was, and they were reluctant to make overly aggressive movements in 1861. By 1862, Johnston had accumulated about forty-five thousand troops total, many of them poorly armed. He was opposed by well-armed Federal troops totaling at least ninety thousand.

CHAPTER 2

War's Brutal Fury: 1862

Early in 1862, Federal forces along the Confederacy's borders began probing. In January a Union force under a tough West Point graduate, Brig. Gen. George H. Thomas, advanced through southeast Kentucky toward Cumberland Gap in an attempt to open a path into eastern Tennessee. On January 19, about four thousand troops under Thomas clashed with an equal number of Confederates north of Mill Springs, Kentucky, at Logan's Cross Roads on Fishing Creek. There Brig. Gen. Felix K. Zollicoffer became the first of Tennessee's generals to be killed in action. The fighting raged back and forth in the midst of a violent rainstorm. During the confusion of close-quarter action, nearsighted General Zollicoffer rode up to a colonel and began shouting orders at him. Unfortunately for Zollicoffer, the officer was Union rather than Confederate, and the colonel promptly leveled a pistol at the surprised general and shot him out of his saddle. The Confederates fought on as best they could; many had outdated flintlock muskets rather than percussion cap rifles like their Northern foes. The Southerners were simply outgunned as the rain rendered the gunpowder in their old muskets' priming pans wet and useless. After three hours of desperate action, the Southern battle line broke as a rousing Union bayonet charge

surged forward. With approximately five hundred casualties, the Confederates were routed; the Federals suffered only about half that number. Suddenly eastern Tennessee was wide open for a Union invasion. However, the rough mountain terrain of the region would still delay the Federal advance.

Meanwhile, to the west, the U.S. Army and Navy launched a joint operation to force open the strategically important Tennessee and Cumberland Rivers in February. If a Federal amphibious force could utilize the two great rivers to advance deep into Middle Tennessee, such a force could cut the region's vital railroad lines and capture the state capital at Nashville. However, there were some alert Confederate authorities who were well aware of what the Federals would attempt to do. Governor Harris had ordered the construction of strong defenses on the rivers near the Kentucky border earlier in the war. Fort Henry was established on the east bank of the

Tennessee River, Fort Donelson twelve miles away on the west bank of the Cumberland. The security of West Tennessee, Nashville, and the region's railroads depended on the ability of the Confederates to hold their two river forts.

The man assigned to command both forts, Brig. Gen. Lloyd Tilghman, was a West Pointer who had been a civil engineer before the war. When he first saw Fort Henry, he was astounded by its poor location. The fort was on such low ground that even an ordinary spring rise of the river level would put much of the post's defenses under water. Nevertheless, there was not enough time to construct a new fort, and Tilghman had to make do with what he had. However, with the help of five hundred slaves, he began work on supplemental defenses located on high ground across the river from Fort Henry, hoping to strengthen his position.

In command of the Federal forces massing against Fort Henry were two men: Brig. Gen. Ulysses S. Grant in charge of the land force, and Flag Officer Andrew H. Foote in charge of the naval squadron. The relatively obscure Grant recently had proved his willingness to fight at the Battle of Belmont, Missouri, on November 7, 1861. A West Point graduate and Mexican War veteran, Grant had had a run of bad luck on failed business ventures after leaving the army. When the war broke out in '61, he volunteered his services; unknown to him or anyone else at the time, within four years he would be a national hero destined for the presidency. For the expedition against Fort Henry, Grant had thousands of troops with which he planned to launch a land assault in conjunction with Foote's naval attack from the river. Andrew Foote was an old saltwater sailor trying to cope with the idea of a freshwater navy on inland rivers. During his adventurous career he had fought Malayan pirates in the East Indies and slavers off the African coast. The gruff naval officer had experienced a shipboard conversion to Christianity and regularly gave fire-and-brimstone sermons to his men, who remained loyal to him in spite of it all. Even when he did away with their traditional ration of grog, his sailors still couldn't hold a grudge against their like-able, grandfatherly commander.

Foote's river fleet for the Fort Henry expedition was destined to make naval history. A new type of warship had been developed by an engineering contractor for the Federal government, James B. Eads. Made to withstand the merciless pounding of the heavy artillery from shore fortifications, as well as the big guns of other ships, Eads's new vessels were known as "ironclads." Sometimes they were built from scratch, but frequently they were made from converted civilian steamboats. Eads's design was simple but effective: after a ship's structure was covered with protective heavy timbers, a layer of thick iron plates was placed over the wood. Foote would have four such revolutionary gunboats to test in battle against Fort Henry. The results would change naval warfare forever.

From their base at Cairo, Illinois, where the Mississippi and Ohio Rivers meet, Grant and Foote formulated their plans. On January 29, 1862, the ambitious Union commanders finally received the official go-ahead from their department commander to take Fort Henry. They immediately moved their base to the Ohio River town of Paducah, Kentucky, situated at the mouth of the Tennessee River (Paducah had been seized by Grant the previous year). On February 2, seven gunboats, including four ironclads, accompanied by a flotilla of steamboats loaded with over half of Grant's seventeen-thousand-man army, shoved off from the river port at Paducah, chugging up the Tennessee River. After unloading the troops as close to Fort Henry as possible, the steamboats were to immediately return to Paducah to bring the balance of the Union force upriver to join their comrades a few days later. Great black clouds billowed from the fleet's numerous smokestacks, alerting the entire countryside of the Federals' steady progress on the river.

At Fort Henry, reports began coming in concerning the large invasion force moving upriver. The five-sided earthwork fort enclosed about three acres and had seventeen artillery pieces. However, as luck would have it, the river was rising, and a portion of the fort was already flooded; some of the stronghold's big guns would soon be submerged. General Tilghman had only about twenty-six hundred troops in and around the post to challenge the overwhelming numbers of Federals packed on the steamboats chugging upriver. He wired his superior, General Johnston, for reinforcements. Tilghman optimistically claimed that with more men he could win a great victory. But enough reinforcements would never come; there would be no Southern victory at Fort Henry.

By February 4, the Union invasion fleet was nearing its objective, and a number of troops were sent ashore. However, Grant decided to personally look over Fort Henry and its surrounding area before landing all his army. He wanted to get his troops as near to the fort as possible without coming within range of its artillery. He steamed upriver, ahead of the main fleet, on the ironclad *Essex* accompanied by two other gunboats. As the small flotilla came within sight of Fort Henry, the gunboats opened fire. Grant and naval commander William Porter stood on the deck of the *Essex* as the big guns of the fort replied with a thunderous salvo. At first the Confederate artillery rounds fell far short of the gunboats, harmlessly spraying river water into the air. Then the fort's big rifled cannon joined the action. Suddenly the little Federal fleet was well within range as huge artillery rounds whistled overhead. One shot very nearly struck Grant and Porter themselves, crashing through the deck and penetrating the cabin before splashing into the river. Thus, Grant had his answer to the question of the fort's artillery range, and the gunboats immediately turned back and steamed out of sight.

The brisk exchange of artillery fire ending with the withdrawal of the Federal gunboats briefly raised Confederate morale at Fort Henry. Yet reality once again set in as General Tilghman and his men considered the odds of winning against a sustained bombardment of their post by seven gunboats, including four ironclads, coupled with a land assault by a force

An artillery shell narrowly missed Grant and Porter as they stood on deck.

that was obviously many times larger than their own. Tilghman's thoughts turned more and more to the idea of abandoning Fort Henry in favor of the bigger, stronger, dryer Fort Donelson. His men from Fort Henry could reinforce the troops already at Donelson, and there, on better ground, they could make a serious, determined stand against Grant's army and Foote's gunboats.

The water was two feet deep at Fort Henry's flagpole by the morning of February 5. The artillery positions at the fort's lowest level would soon be flooded. General Tilghman turned to his chief of artillery, Capt. Jesse Taylor, and asked if he could hold out for one hour against the Federal assault. The artillery captain gave a positive reply, and Tilghman decided to march all but about a hundred of his troops to Fort Donelson. The few brave defenders left behind at Fort Henry would delay the Federal invaders long enough for twenty-five hundred Confederate soldiers to escape. Tilghman led away his poorly armed troops who struggled along the muddy road to Donelson as they shouldered their old flintlock muskets, relics of the War of 1812. Then, with his troops well on their way, the heroic Tilghman and some of his staff turned back to make a hopeless stand at Fort Henry with the other few unlucky defenders.

On the morning of February 6, the long-awaited attack on Fort Henry commenced with Grant's troops starting their march on both sides of the river. One column moved to seize the fortified heights opposite Fort Henry (which had, in fact, already been abandoned by the Confederates), and one column advanced to cut the Southerners' escape route (too late to stop the twenty-five hundred marching to Fort Donelson). Foote's gunboats steamed upriver as the land force advanced, prepared for their bold assault. However, the Federal plan soon fell apart as Grant's troops encountered deep mud and high water in stream beds that mercilessly delayed their progress. Foote's fleet was destined to fight the battle without the mud-choked army.

The ironclads chugged upriver and formed four abreast, with the *Cincinnati, Carondelet, St. Louis,* and *Essex* all in a neat line with their bows pointed toward the fort. The other three gunboats, timberclads (protected by heavy timbers but no iron plates), followed close behind. At a distance of seventeen hundred yards from the fort, Flag Officer Foote, aboard the *Cincinnati,* gave the command to open fire. The first three shots fell short, but the Federals soon got the correct range of the fortifications, and their marksmanship proved deadly. Inside the fort, Captain Taylor had assigned each of his twelve serviceable guns a specific boat as a target. When the vessels were about a mile away, the Confederate artillery pieces cut loose with a roaring salvo. Taylor's big guns blazed away from behind the fort's eight-foot-high, fourteen-foot-wide parapets. Meanwhile, Grant's troops, still struggling through the mud and brush, felt adrenaline rush through their veins as they heard the thunderous battle ahead of them grow in fierce intensity. The dramatic duel between the gunboats and the flooded fort continued as cannon thunder rolled across the Tennessee River. Soon Foote's fleet was within only six hundred yards of Tilghman's gunsmoke-shrouded defenses.

Suddenly a solid shot tore through the iron plating and oak support of the *Essex* and entered the casemate where its steam boilers were located. The projectile ripped a large hole in the center boiler, and an explosion of scalding steam and boiling water engulfed the forward gun deck, sending screaming sailors rushing to the ports to throw themselves overboard. The disabled *Essex* drifted downriver with ten dead, twenty-three wounded, and five missing in the muddy river water. Among the badly wounded was Commander Porter. Tilghman's troops cheered aloud as they saw the *Essex*, engulfed by clouds of steam, drift harmlessly out of the action. Yet before their cheers died down, disaster struck the fort as its big rifled artillery piece burst with a deafening roar, killing its gunnery sergeant and disabling the rest of the crew. Moments later, the fort's second most powerful gun was accidentally spiked when its priming pick broke off in the vent, rendering it useless. The two big guns had broken and scattered numerous iron plates on their foes' gunboats, yet suddenly they were harmless and silent.

Flag Officer Foote continued to draw closer to the fort even as his flagship, the *Cincinnati,* was riddled by destructive fire, receiving thirty-one hits. Two of his artillery pieces were disabled, one being struck by a projectile squarely on its muzzle. Nine of the *Cincinnati'*s crew fell as casualties, but only one shot proved fatal as a tar's head was carried away by a whistling projectile. The three dauntless ironclads closed within three hundred yards of the fort, point-blank range for artillery. The *Carondelet* fired 107 times, and she in turn was struck nine or ten times, becoming interlocked with the *St. Louis* during the action because of the tight spacing of the gunboats' formation. The *St. Louis* fired 116 projectiles, more than any of her sister gunboats, and was hit seven times but suffered no casualties.

The three timberclad gunboats, astern of the line of ironclads, were in relatively little danger once the fort's rifled gun exploded. Captain Taylor's busy gunners scored fifty-nine hits on the Federal fleet during the short but savage battle for Fort Henry. General Tilghman himself threw aside his officer's frock coat and personally helped man one of the guns as more and more artillerymen fell wounded or exhausted. The powerful Dahlgren guns of the ironclads were sweeping the mangled parapets of Fort Henry, throwing great clods of dirt and sandbags into the air. Thunderclap explosions spread deadly havoc among the Confederate defenses, disabling numerous guns and their crews.

After a hellacious bombardment lasting more than an hour, only four of Fort Henry's artillery pieces remained in action. At last General Tilghman told Captain Taylor that the time had come to surrender. The blazing artillery duel on the Tennessee River had lasted for at least seventy-five minutes when the Confederate colors were lowered from Fort Henry's flagstaff. A white banner was raised over the shattered defenses as the guns finally fell silent, and their hazy fog of sulfurous smoke gradually drifted away downstream. A small, white yawl rowed out from the smoking fort (several wooden structures had been set ablaze by the bombardment) with Tilghman's adjutant and another Southern officer. They headed for the *Cincinnati* and told Foote that Tilghman wished to communicate with him. Foote gave Tilghman permission to come aboard but at the same time sent a couple of naval officers in a launch to take possession of the fort. They rowed through the flooded main gate and past the underwater cannons to raise the Stars and Stripes over the wreckage of the vanquished Confederate stronghold. The post's surgeon could be seen frantically treating the fort's casualties. Five soldiers were beyond treatment, dead at their posts; eleven others were wounded; five were missing; and the rest lay exhausted, waiting to become prisoners of war. General Tilghman was escorted to the *Cincinnati* where he is reported to have said to Foote, "I

Henry Wager Halleck

am glad to surrender to so gallant an officer." Foote simply replied that Tilghman had done the right thing to surrender, "but you should have blown my boat out of the water before I would have surrendered, to you."

General Grant arrived at Fort Henry about an hour after the surrender. He had ridden ahead of his mud-choked army when the guns ceased firing in order to find out what had happened. That afternoon he sent a short telegraph to his department commander, Maj. Gen. Henry W. Halleck: "Fort Henry is ours, I shall take and destroy Fort Donelson on the 8th." Halleck wired the succinct message concerning Fort Henry's fall to Washington but did not mention plans for Fort Donelson. Thus, the United States was able to celebrate its first truly strategic victory of the war. Although it had involved only a small number of combatants, had lasted only about an hour, and had produced relatively few casualties, the Battle of Fort Henry was a major triumph for the Union. Its meaning was profound: Confederate general Albert Sidney Johnston's dreaded Tennessee line of defense had been breached. The Federal victory had been accomplished by the bold use of the innovative new iron-plated warship, the ironclad. Henceforth, the Southerners would have a well-founded fear of the slow-moving, deadly gunboats and would build some of their own versions to battle the U.S. Navy.

Grant's plans to advance immediately on Fort Donelson had to be delayed a few days while Foote took his battle-damaged ironclads to Cairo, Illinois, for repairs. Besides, it was to Grant's advantage to delay his advance for awhile because Halleck was sending an additional ten thousand troops as reinforcements. In the meantime, at Grant's request, Lt. Comdr. S. L. Phelps took the three timberclad gunboats farther up the Tennessee River on a destructive little raid. Phelps disabled the bridge of the vital Memphis and Ohio Railroad, burned or captured nine Confederate vessels, and pushed as far south as Florence, Alabama.

While the main actions of the war in Tennessee raged in the west, occasional partisan skirmishing continued in the eastern portion of the state in early 1862. John Hammonds, a trooper in the First East Tennessee Cavalry Regiment, wrote a letter to his uncle describing such a skirmish near Knoxville on February 2: "We had a small chunk of a fight with the Lincolnit[es] the 2 day of this instant. We killed six of them and taken one prisoner and wounded ten more. Jack Thomas a colored person that belongs to our company killed one of them. . . ." The reference to an African-American serving in a Confederate unit was not extremely unusual, especially in a Tennessee outfit. Countless Tennessee volunteers took their "man servants" to war with them. Although they were not officially mustered in as real soldiers, such slaves were welcomed into Confederate military units as teamsters, cooks, horse handlers, camp laborers, etc. They were frequently uniformed and equipped like the regulars, although the Confederate Congress in Richmond did not approve of the official

Pierre Gustave Toutant Beauregard

recruitment of Black soldiers until the war was nearly over. The Tennessee State Library and Archives in Nashville has records on microfilm of 267 Black Confederate Civil War pension applications.

Meanwhile, General Johnston held a council of war at his headquarters in Bowling Green, Kentucky, the day after Fort Henry fell. Among the officers present was his new second-in-command, Gen. Pierre Gustave Toutant Beauregard, Confederate hero of Fort Sumter and Manassas. The Louisiana Frenchman had quarreled with Pres. Jefferson Davis over the conduct of the war, and consequently Davis had transferred him to the West. As a result of this meeting of Western Confederate brass, Johnston began withdrawing his forces from Kentucky, south toward Nashville. He also sent twelve thousand troops to reinforce Fort Donelson, along with a new commander, Brig. Gen. John B. Floyd. Unfortunately, Floyd was simply a politician, not a military man. He had been governor of Virginia and had served as U.S. secretary of war under Pres. James Buchanan. While secretary of war during the early days of impending secession, he had transferred large amounts of U.S. military ordnance south. He was also suspected (probably wrongfully) of misappropriating $870,000 of government funds. His greatest fear was being captured by Federal authorities and put on trial for treasonous acts. Floyd's second-in-command was Brig. Gen. Gideon J. Pillow, a Tennessee lawyer and politician who had served as an officer in the Mexican War. He had been roughed up by Grant at the Battle of Belmont, Missouri, the previous November. Grant had known Pillow during the Mexican War, and as a result he had absolutely no respect for Pillow's martial prowess. Next in command at Fort Donelson was a man of greater military ability, Brig. Gen. Simon Bolivar Buckner, a former West Point classmate of Grant's. They had served in the Mexican War together. Buckner had even loaned his former school chum money during Grant's hard times in civilian life.

This awkward triumvirate of Confederate brigadiers commanded a fortified enclosure of a hundred acres atop a plateau on the Cumberland River. Their fort was next to the village of Dover, consisting of a courthouse, several houses, and a two-story inn and tavern named the Dover Hotel, where the three generals set up their headquarters. Beneath the stronghold's bluff above the riverbank were two powerful artillery batteries covering the approach from the river. Outside the fort, along the ridges that enclosed it, were trenches and log defenses packed with earth. Beyond the earthworks were hillsides covered with felled trees, chopped down for two purposes: to clear a field of fire, and to create obstructions to slow an advancing foe. Floyd, Pillow, and Buckner had seventeen thousand troops under their command. One of their cavalry officers would prove to be especially battleworthy for the Southern Cause. The semi-literate former slave trader and planter had risen from private to lieutenant colonel and was destined to reach higher rank and prominence before the war

Nathan Bedford Forrest

was over. Lieutenant Colonel Nathan Bedford Forrest was a man who possessed a fearsome inborn military ability.

The Union force General Grant was amassing against Fort Donelson would eventually number twenty-seven thousand troops. His army was divided into three divisions under, coincidentally, three brigadier generals: Charles F. Smith, a veteran of the regular army and Grant's former West Point commandant; John A. McClernand, an Illinois lawyer and former member of Congress; and Lew Wallace, who would later author the popular novel *Ben Hur* and become governor of New Mexico Territory. Also Grant would once again have the assistance of Flag Officer Foote and his fleet of gunboats.

The U.S. infantry divisions of Smith and McClernand marched across the Tennessee countryside on February 12, reaching the outer works of Fort Donelson before noon. The weather was mild, and many of the troops discarded their heavy overcoats and blankets, thinking spring had come early. In the distance, they could hear the rumble of cannon fire along the river. The ironclad *Carondelet* exchanged a few shots with the fort's water batteries, then chugged out of gun range. Grant spent the rest of the day directing an encirclement of the fort's land defenses as the sporadic crack of sharpshooters' rifles filled the air.

On the morning of the thirteenth, Grant continued his envelopment of the Confederate land defenses except for an open space left in the center of the Union line which would be filled by General Wallace's division upon its arrival the next day. The Union artillery was now well in place, and the numerous bronze cannons began a thunderous bombardment of the fort with the Confederates' big guns responding defiantly. One Confederate battery on a well-fortified hill proved to be particularly bothersome to General McClernand's position. The politician-turned-general ordered three of his regiments to launch an assault on the hill without proper authorization from Grant. His Illinois troops surged forward, and many were soon cut down by a horrific crossfire from the battery they were trying to take and two others on adjoining hills. Then as the survivors drew closer to their goal, a long line of Rebel muskets burst into flame, sending a storm of lead into the ranks of the blue-coated soldiers. Three times they bravely charged up the hill only to be driven back by a deadly rain of canister balls and bullets. By the third assault, numerous dry leaves had been ignited by the heavy gunfire, and brush fires swept the field. Flames engulfed screaming wounded soldiers lying helpless on the battlefield as the sun set in the west.

The north wind had begun to blow and brought with it sleet and snow. During the night, the temperature dropped to ten degrees, and many of the wounded who had escaped the brushfires froze to death. The Federal troops who had discarded the extra weight of their overcoats and blankets now suffered miserably. To squat by a campfire was dangerous business—it invited Confederate sharpshooters to show off their marksmanship. Many Union soldiers would remember this as their worst night of the entire war.

In the early morning darkness of February 14, new hope for the Union Cause arrived. Flag Officer Andrew Foote's flotilla of five gunboats, including three ironclads, and twelve army transports carrying ten thousand reinforcements from General Halleck, chugged up the river and tied up three miles below Fort Donelson. Most of the ten thousand troops were assigned to Gen. Lew Wallace, who also arrived with two thousand additional men from captured Fort Henry. The Union army was now twenty-seven thousand strong. Grant strengthened his ring around the fort's land defenses and requested that Foote attack immediately from the Cumberland River. Foote reluctantly agreed. The only reconnaissance information he had about the fort was provided by Capt. Henry Walke of the ironclad *Carondelet*, which had been present early and had traded shots briefly with the Confederate water batteries on the twelfth. Grant and Foote both hoped for a repeat of the Fort Henry victory, but dry Fort Donelson was defended by more powerful guns than was Henry. Nevertheless, Foote spent the morning preparing his fleet for battle.

Foote's gunboats hove into the Cumberland River's floodwaters beneath Fort Donelson at 1:45 P.M. Up the river they came in a grim battle line with the *Louisville* on the west flank, then Foote's flag steamer the *St. Louis,* then the *Pittsburgh,* and on the east end of the line, the *Carondelet.* Two wooden gunboats chugged behind the wall of ironclads. The crusty old saltwater sailor Foote occasionally popped out of his pilothouse on the *St. Louis* with his old-fashioned officer's hailing trumpet (an early type of megaphone) to bellow orders for his vessels to maintain their alignment. Close to 3:00 P.M., at a range of less than two thousand yards, the gunboats fired their first long-range salvo at the fort, whose water batteries held their fire, waiting for the flotilla to come closer. As the ironclads closed to within about a thousand yards of the batteries' earthworks, the firing suddenly grew in intensity as the Confederates' two largest guns opened up on the little Union fleet. Foote urged his vessels onward, closer to the Confederate defenses, until they were within just four hundred yards. At that distance, his entire fleet was within range of all twelve Confederate cannons facing the river. Foote's gunners had to raise their cannon barrels to maximum elevation since the Rebel river batteries loomed above them. The big guns on both sides now spoke their loud, deadly dialogue of war, spouting forth smoke and flame as their ominous thunder reverberated along the banks of the Cumberland. The solid iron shot hurled by the fort's guns slammed into the gunboats' armor and made a continuous ringing sound up and down the river as though a huge blacksmith's forge was in full operation in the middle of a great thunderstorm.

The continuous boom of artillery and shriek of shells hurtling through the smoky air was deafening. Many of the gunboats' rounds overshot the Confederate defenses as they were fired from elevated barrels sending the projectiles in a high arc. Meanwhile, the marksmanship of the Southerners was beginning to take a toll on the Union fleet. All four ironclads were taking a terrific pounding as armor plates were busted and torn away; smokestacks were shot off; and flagstaffs, chains, and lines were severed. Numerous sailors fell victim to both exploding shells and solid shot as the deadly projectiles tore their way into and through the bowels of the gunboats, throwing chunks of iron and wooden splinters everywhere. Captain Walke of the *Carondelet* described the hail of destructive artillery projectiles "tearing off the side armor as lightning tears the bark from a tree." Foote's tactic of close range, ship-to-shore combat, which had worked at Fort Henry, was now failing at Fort Donelson, which had much greater firepower than her little sister fort. Suddenly a huge shell crashed into the pilothouse of the *St. Louis,* killing the pilot, carrying away the wheel, and leaving Foote himself painfully wounded in the ankle. His flag steamer now drifted downstream, out of control behind the *Louisville,* which had also been disabled when her rudder chains and tiller were severed. Meanwhile, the *Pittsburgh* and the *Carondelet* had their hulls breached by the terrific bombardment and were both taking on water. The *Pittsburgh* was in danger of sinking bow first until her captain shifted all the weight of his guns to the stern of the boat. As the off-balance *Pittsburgh* then turned in the river, she collided with the *Carondelet,* shearing off Captain Walke's rudder. The *Carondelet* then drifted downstream backward with her bow guns blazing away defiantly, screening her escape with a fog of gunsmoke. Cheer after cheer arose from the Confederate defenses as the victorious Southerners watched the U.S. Navy drift harmlessly away to care for its casualties and repair the heavy damages inflicted by Fort Donelson's powerful river defenses.

Confederate morale soared high within the defenses of Fort Donelson. They had whipped the ironclads and had thrown back the Federal ground forces the day before. But their enemy did not go away. The nervous triumvirate of Confederate brigadiers met and decided their next course of action. They correctly analyzed that their military situation called for a long, miserable siege by the Federal forces, which was exactly what General Grant was then preparing for. The three brigadiers chose a bold course of action: they would execute a breakout by land beginning with a massive assault on the Union lines and ending with a march to Nashville by their army. Their forces would conduct an orderly, fighting retreat all the way southeast to the great Southern city where they would unite with General Johnston and his army. Inside the fort, the troops spent the night preparing for an attack at dawn.

General Grant left the Union lines before dawn on the fateful day of February 15, 1862, to confer with Flag Officer Foote who was recovering from his wound at his anchorage several miles below Fort Donelson. Before leaving, Grant did not designate a second-in-command and issued orders for his division commanders to hold their positions. At dawn, Generals Pillow and Buckner ordered their poorly armed troops out of the fort's defenses to smash the Federal right under luckless

General McClernand. However, they didn't catch the Yanks napping. The night had been too cold for sleep, and the tired bluecoats were already up milling around when the bone-chilling Rebel yell broke the frosty morning silence, and the tearing crash of musket volleys pierced the winter air. For about three hours the struggle raged on the Federal right with McClernand's division stubbornly giving ground, foot by foot, to the massive Southern assault. Frantic attempts were made to locate Grant and have him rescind his order (for everyone to hold their position) so that McClernand's men could be reinforced by troops from the other divisions. Finally, Lew Wallace disobeyed orders by commanding some of his troops to leave their position and reinforce the Federal right. He acted just in time to save McClernand from total disaster as his men ran out of ammunition. Yet it was too late to plug the gap that had been punched in the Union line. The knockout blow was delivered to the Federals by Lt. Col. Nathan Bedford Forrest who led his cavalry troopers in a dismounted assault on the extreme right flank of McClernand's line. Suddenly there was a hole in the Federal line that was big enough to march an army through. The Confederate attack had achieved its objective; the road to Nashville was open!

Yet as General Pillow rode among his victorious troops, he was overcome by the ugly aftermath of a major armed clash. He saw many of his men bleeding and screaming in pain. Those who were not casualties were exhausted and low on ammunition. He saw numerous dead scattered in grotesque positions where they had fallen across the torn landscape of the smoky battlefield. The general was overcome by the hideous scene and decided this was not a force that could survive a freezing march to Nashville while withstanding attacks by the Union army along the way. Pillow did not have the hardened heart of a warrior; he ordered all the Southern troops back to the safety of Donelson's trenches. Flabbergasted, Buckner at first refused to obey. Now was the time to march southeast to Nashville, he thought. Those unable to march

would simply have to be left behind. There was no time for pity
and mercy; the march must be made now or never! Yet it was
never to be made. Indecisive General Floyd, who rode forward
after the combat, was at first also astounded by Pillow's order,
yet then agreed with him. Buckner, the obedient soldier, reluctantly did as his superiors ordered.

Meanwhile, General Grant had finally arrived on the battlefield. He had spurred his horse on a gallop over seven miles of
icy road after an aide had at last reached him with news of the
Confederate surprise attack. Frustrated, he crumpled papers
in his hand as he listened to McClernand and Wallace describe
the disaster that had befallen them. Grant then scrawled an
order to be taken back to Foote calling for support from the
damaged gunboats. Then he gained his composure and sternly refused to panic. He quickly assessed the situation, taking
note of the report that all the Confederate dead appeared to
have three day's worth of rations in their haversacks. Grant
correctly analyzed the meaning of this fact. The realization of
what then needed to be done must have struck him like a thun-
derbolt. In that instant, he was transformed from an obscure,
ordinary fellow into a man of great destiny. His decision would
propel him to the status of a national hero. Grant turned to a
member of his staff and said, "Some of our men are pretty
badly demoralized, but the enemy must be more so, for he has
attempted to force his way out, but has fallen back: the one
who attacks first now will be victorious, and the enemy will
have to be in a hurry if he gets ahead of me."

Grant rode to the Federal left and told Gen. C. F. Smith, "All
has failed on our right. You must take Fort Donelson." Grant
knew that the Confederates defending the earthworks before
Smith's division must have been depleted in numbers to support the main Southern assault on the other end of the line.
He also knew the tough old veteran officer Smith would not
hesitate to carry out his order. With his long white mustache
blowing in the winter wind, General Smith personally led his
division in a furious charge against the Rebel defenses before

The tough old veteran C. F. Smith did not hesitate to carry out the order to charge.

him. The single regiment Buckner had left to hold the line on the Confederate right, the Thirtieth Tennessee, poured a deadly hail of lead into the advancing ranks of Iowa troops. The Yanks moved steadily forward with their bayonets bristling like a fearsome phalanx. Many a brave young Iowa soldier fell, yet the gaps they left were immediately filled by others as the long blue line surged forward.

The overwhelming numbers of Federal bayonets forced the sparse Tennessee troops out of their earthworks. Then for two desperate hours, General Buckner attempted to retake the defenses with repeated furious charges by reinforcements he brought from the Confederate left. But Smith and his men would not budge from their captured prize. In the distance, the rumble of artillery on the river could be heard as Foote carried out Grant's earlier order for support from the gunboats. Meanwhile, the new man of destiny ordered an advance on his right to reclaim the ground lost in the morning surprise attack. By nightfall, the relentless Federal army had dug in with a better position than they had possessed at the start of the bloody day.

That evening, at the Dover Hotel, the Confederate leaders held a council of war. Buckner was severely despondent. Floyd and Pillow, in their ignorance of military matters, at first were still optimistic over the morning surprise attack's initial success. Buckner brought them down to the cold hard facts of reality. The Federals were now within the outer defenses on the Confederate right. The Union army had regained the ground they lost in the morning on the Confederate left. The Southerners were still greatly outnumbered and exhausted from constant combat; they were in no shape to withstand a massive U.S. assault the following day. Buckner scolded Pillow and Floyd, railing that they should have marched out when the gap was opened in the Federal line that morning. Now, he said, all was lost. By 1:00 A.M. the three brigadiers were discussing surrender, and they summoned Lt. Col. Nathan B. Forrest. The cavalry commander was astounded that they would consider capitulating to the Yankees. He presented several options: the Federals, he claimed, had not occupied their extreme right by the river, and he believed a way out was still open there; or they could once again fight their way out, and he guaranteed to cover their rear with his hard-fighting troopers; also his men had found a little-used river road that was still open despite being submerged by three-foot-deep, ice-cold

Forrest, Buckner, Floyd, and Pillow faced the hard decision.

floodwater for about a hundred yards. The generals were unimpressed; plans for surrender continued. Forrest stomped out of the room in disgust growling, "I did not come here for the purpose of surrendering my command." The fearless cavalry officer then proceeded to escape successfully with his entire regiment, and a number of infantrymen, on the flooded river road he had described. Meanwhile, back at the council of war, Generals Floyd and Pillow agreed that surrender was the only option left, but they themselves did not wish to be part of it, preferring to sneak out rather than become prisoners of war. Floyd passed his command to Pillow who, in turn, passed it to Buckner. The man who should have been in command of Fort Donelson all along was at last in charge. But this change in command came much too late, and the plans made at the Dover Hotel that night called for Confederate surrender.

Before dawn on February 16, 1862, General Floyd commandeered two steamboats docked nearby and escaped downriver with about fifteen hundred of his Virginia troops. Meanwhile, General Pillow and his staff successfully escaped across the river in a skiff. Shortly after dawn, General Buckner sent a message to General Grant under a white flag, proposing that they discuss surrender terms. Grant's famous reply was to be printed in every newspaper across the divided nation: "No terms except an unconditional and immediate surrender can be accepted. I propose to move immediately on your works." To an admiring Northern public, Ulysses Simpson Grant became "Unconditional Surrender" Grant, a great American hero. To a depressed Southern public, he gained recognition as one of their most dangerous enemies. Buckner surrendered an estimated twelve to thirteen thousand troops to Grant. Of the original seventeen thousand defenders of Fort Donelson, about five hundred were killed, approximately a thousand wounded were evacuated before the surrender, and two thousand or more escaped by the river or through the Union lines. Federal casualties in dead and wounded were nearly identical to their foes: 510 killed, 2,152 wounded.

In a sense, there was one more Union casualty of the battle for Fort Donelson—General Grant himself. Newspaper accounts mentioned that he had fought at Donelson with a cigar clamped in his teeth. Soon, admirers from across the Federal Union were sending him countless boxes of cigars. As a result, Grant, who had only occasionally indulged in tobacco, became a cigar chain smoker till the end of his days in 1885 when he died of throat cancer. Ironically, among his last visitors before his death was his old army buddy from the Mexican War, the friend who had loaned him money when he was down and out, the Confederate general who had surrendered Fort Donelson: Simon B. Buckner.

In Nashville, Gen. Albert Sidney Johnston received news of the surrender of Fort Donelson a short time later that same morning. As Sunday church bells were ringing, Johnston advised Governor Harris to make arrangements to move his state government; the Confederate army was abandoning Nashville. Johnston's troops and wagons lumbered through the streets of Nashville to their eventual destination at Corinth, a railroad junction in northern Mississippi. There they would regroup and join with other Southern forces to prepare for a massive counterattack on the Union army. Thus, the great Southern city of Nashville fell into Northern hands. The flag of the United States once again flew over the state capitol building as Tennessee's Confederate government retreated to Memphis. Andrew Johnson, the senator from Tennessee who had refused to secede, was commissioned a brigadier general and appointed military governor of the state by the Federal government.

Meanwhile, another Federal army, other than Grant's, was on the march from Bowling Green, Kentucky. Brigadier General Don Carlos Buell and his Army of the Ohio (named after the Ohio River) had been ordered to occupy Nashville and stand ready to cooperate with Grant in future operations. However, the aggressive Grant personally arrived in Nashville before Buell. Major General Henry Halleck, Grant's superior, frowned on his subordinate's unbridled aggressiveness and in a show of petty jealousy and fear for his own personal ambitions, suspended Grant from command and ordered him to await further instructions at Fort Henry. Halleck replaced Grant with one of his division commanders, the gallant Gen.

Charles F. Smith. Halleck also began to attempt to discredit Grant in Washington, saying that he had "resumed his former bad habits" (a reference to Grant's fondness for whiskey). However, President Lincoln, the shrewd and tactful politician, helped put an end to Halleck's spiteful smear campaign. He recognized Grant as a military talent that the nation sorely needed and promoted him to major general. But to pacify Halleck, he gave him what he had long wished for, overall command of Federal forces in the West.

Meanwhile, with General Smith in command, the Army of the Tennessee (as the U.S. force became known) moved up the Tennessee to a small river port called Pittsburg Landing. There the army prepared for an attack on Johnston's Confederate army at Corinth, Mississippi, just twenty-two miles to the southwest. Halleck also ordered Buell to march his Army of the Ohio to Savannah, Tennessee, a small town nine miles downstream from Pittsburg Landing. Suddenly the hand of fate seemed to intervene as General Smith received a serious leg injury and had to give up his command. Grant was restored to duty and sent to Savannah with orders to concentrate troops and supplies but not to bring on a general engagement until both the Army of Tennessee and the Army of the Ohio were united and Halleck himself had arrived to assume personal command of the combined forces. However, Grant's next armed clash with the Confederates would not be of his own choosing.

At Corinth, Gen. Albert S. Johnston and Gen. P. G. T. Beauregard worked feverishly to assemble, arm, train, and supply the great Confederate army with which they planned to crush Federal ambitions in the Western Theater; the forty-four-thousand-man Army of the Mississippi was organized and readied for combat. Its four corps commanders were illustrious men of the South: Maj. Gen. Braxton Bragg, who had gained national fame during the Mexican War as well as the personal friendship of Jefferson Davis; Maj. Gen. William J. Hardee, who was a career soldier and author of *Hardee's Tactics*, a military

Braxton Bragg

manual of drill and tactics used by the armies of both sides throughout the war; Brig. Gen. John C. Breckinridge, former vice president of the United States; and Maj. Gen. Leonidas Polk, bishop of the Episcopal Church in Louisiana, who was also a West Point graduate. Johnston and his generals planned to launch a devastating surprise attack on Grant's Army of the Tennessee at Pittsburg Landing.

Johnston received reports that Buell and his Army of the Ohio were drawing near to Savannah, Tennessee, and decided the time had come to attack Grant's Army of the Tennessee before it could unite with Buell's force. Johnston issued the order to march northeast on April 3. He planned to give battle on April 5, but heavy rains and bad roads made progress slow, and Confederate plans were changed. Johnston and his Army of the Mississippi camped only about two miles away from Pittsburg Landing on the night of April 5. They would advance in the early morning hours before dawn on April 6.

General Grant did not expect an attack and spent Saturday night, April 5, at the Cherry Mansion in Savannah, where

Union headquarters had been set up. His army had been encamped at Pittsburg Landing for two weeks and, unfortunately for the Federals, no entrenchments had been dug. As a matter of fact, it was a common military theory at the time that having troops dig defenses tended to demoralize them. Instead, the troops spent their time in constant training, subjected to continuous drill, which they badly needed. Many of the soldiers were green recruits who initially didn't even know how to properly load a rifle. Their drill instruction was soon to pay off.

During Grant's absence, he had left the Pittsburg Landing encampment under the command of one of his division commanders, the dependable Brig. Gen. William Tecumseh Sherman, a veteran of Bull Run. Sherman's raw recruits in his own division held the advance position about four miles inland from the river landing on the right of the Federal line of countless tents. Sherman had set up his headquarters near a crossroads and a one-room log cabin constructed by Methodists a decade earlier for church services. The little meetinghouse was given the biblical name of Shiloh, meaning "place of peace." To the left of this division was another under the command of Brig. Gen. Benjamin M. Prentiss, a veteran of the Mexican War and a lawyer from Illinois. Together, these two divisions would form the Federal front line. To the rear of Sherman's camp was the division of Brig. Gen. Stephen A. Hurlbut, who was originally from South Carolina but had moved to Illinois to practice law. To the rear, almost at the river landing itself, was Maj. Gen. Charles F. Smith's well-trained division of Fort Donelson veterans, now under the command of Brig. Gen. William H. L. Wallace. A sixth division, under the command of Maj. Gen. Lew Wallace, was encamped at Crump's Landing, about halfway between Savannah and Pittsburg Landing. In all, by April 5, there were in the five U.S. divisions encamped by Pittsburg Landing: 39,830 troops present for duty and an additional 7,564 in the division at Crump's Landing.

In the early morning darkness of Sunday, April 6, 1862, the great Confederate army of about forty-four thousand men began its advance in order of battle toward Pittsburg Landing. It was only six days short of an entire year since Fort Sumter, South Carolina, had been fired upon. Now a tremendous storm of battle, unlike any ever experienced before on the North American continent, was to shake the earth around a little log Tennessee church called Shiloh.

Many accounts of the Battle of Shiloh exaggerate how surprised the Federals were as the assault began. Some accounts have them still asleep in their tents or eating breakfast as they are suddenly overrun. If this were truly the case, then the battle would no doubt be remembered as an overwhelming Confederate victory that lasted only a few hours one morning. Actually, an alert reconnoitering party of Union troops, three companies of the Twenty-Fifth Missouri Infantry Regiment under Maj. James Powell, encountered the skirmish line of the Confederate force a short distance in front of Sherman's camps at about 5:00 A.M. A brisk exchange of gunfire in the early morning darkness ensued with the stubborn Missourians giving ground slowly, refusing to panic. With the help of reinforcements, the small Federal detachment kept up a steady fire that alerted the huge Union encampment. An entire brigade soon came to their rescue, and the Confederate surprise attack was held in check until about 8:00 A.M.

General Sherman rode forward with his aide to investigate soon after the shooting began. Immediately, his aide was shot dead from his saddle, and Sherman was wounded in the hand. Union officers shouted commands as their troops frantically grabbed their weapons and fell into formation. However by 8:00 A.M., the full might of the Confederate army surged forward. They seemed unstoppable as they overran the camps of Sherman and Prentiss. Private Sam Watkins of the First Tennessee Infantry recalled the scene as his regiment advanced in support of an Alabama brigade: "The air was full of balls and deadly missiles. The litter corps was carrying off the dying and wounded. We could hear the shout of the charge and the incessant roar of the guns, the rattle of the musketry, and knew that the contending forces were engaged in a breast to breast struggle."

General Grant was at breakfast in the Cherry Mansion in Savannah when he heard a distant thunder. He went onto the porch and listened for a moment. As a veteran soldier, he recognized the ominous rumble of embattled artillery and knew at once that his camps at Pittsburg Landing were under attack. He and his staff immediately boarded his headquarters steamboat *Tigress,* which was standing by. While waiting for the vessel to get its steam up, Grant dispatched orders for General Buell to bring up reinforcements to Pittsburg Landing. Buell's army had begun arriving at Savannah the day before. Thus, Confederate general Johnston had failed to attack Pittsburg Landing before Buell's army arrived in the area. This critical fact ensured defeat for the South at Shiloh.

Meanwhile, Generals Sherman and McClernand partially stabilized the situation on the right of the Federal battle line and began an orderly fighting withdrawal, stubbornly giving ground to the overwhelming numbers of Rebel troops. Sherman's actions were especially noteworthy that morning. With a handkerchief wrapped around his wounded hand, he cooly directed his troops in the thick of battle and had four horses shot out from under him. When Grant's aide-de-camp arrived to inform him that his commander had arrived on the field, he found Sherman dismounted and standing boldly upright, observing the battle under heavy fire as everyone around him nervously crouched down. Sherman calmly but sternly requested that Grant send him more troops if he could spare them.

As General Grant arrived on the battlefield, General Prentiss's line on the Federal left was about to crumble. A dramatic Confederate bayonet charge swept across three hundred yards of open ground and pushed Prentiss's troops back to their tents. Soon after, Prentiss's division was forced out of its

The aide found Sherman intensely watching the battle, oblivious to the gunfire.

camp and completely routed. As the temporarily victorious Rebels reached the Yankee camps, they stopped to wolf down food they found around the campfires. Some of the hungry Southerners had not eaten in twenty-four hours. They also grabbed souvenirs. When General Johnston himself rode into the captured camp, he stopped to rebuke one of his officers he saw emerging from a tent with an armful of plunder. But seeing the look of dismay on his loyal soldier's face, Johnston paused and then suddenly leaned over in his saddle, grabbed a tin cup off a Union camp table, and jovially declared, "Let this be my share of the spoils today!" Sheathing his sword, he began to wave the tin cup in its place as he gave orders.

The pause in the battle which resulted from the Confederates' plunder of the Union camps gave General Prentiss valuable time to regroup. He gathered together the remnants of his command, initially perhaps only a thousand troops, and formed them into a line of battle on an old wagon road about a mile behind their original position. It was slightly sunken from innumerable years of use but was actually located on high ground and fringed with brush. A great deal of the area Prentiss occupied also commanded a huge open field. Attacking troops would have to pass over this field and break through the brush, as well as a strong rail fence, to get to Prentiss and his men. On the flanks of Prentiss's force, two fresh divisions from the rear of the Federal line came forward. Then Sherman and McClernand aligned their troops on the right of these forces. Thus, a new Federal battle line was formed about 10:30 A.M.

When General Grant rode forward to consult with Sherman, he found the fiery, redheaded warrior worried about running out of ammunition. Grant told him more was on its way and rode off to check the rest of the line. Grant's aide then commented about the worsening situation, and his commander optimistically replied that Lew Wallace's division should soon be arriving. Earlier that morning, as Grant was heading toward Pittsburg Landing aboard the *Tigress,* he had stopped briefly at Crump's Landing to tell General Wallace to get his division ready to move. Now as the lull in the battle came to an end and the horrific human tide of Southern manhood surged forward once more toward the nervous Union battle line, Wallace's division would be sorely missed. Throughout the rest of the bloody first day of battle at Shiloh, Grant and his desperate soldiers would anxiously await the arrival of both Lew Wallace's division and Buell's Army of the Ohio.

With renewed fury, the Southerners struck the new Federal battle line like a sledgehammer. A series of massed frontal assaults took place all along the three-and-a-half-mile-long line as a dense fog of gunsmoke settled over the battlefield's forbidding landscape. General Johnston wanted to push hardest on the Federal left so as to cut his enemy off from Pittsburg Landing. Without that base of supply and avenue of escape, Johnston hoped Grant's army would crumble under his repeated assaults. About noon Johnston rode to his line's extreme right (the Federals' left) to personally direct the Confederate operations in that critical area. Pinned down by horrific fire from Union general Hurlbut's division, the Confederate troops prepared for a massive charge ordered by Johnston. Tennessee governor Isham Harris rode by Johnston's side, bravely serving as his aide and courier in the fierce battle. He recalled how Johnston's personal charisma spurred the men to action as he walked his horse Fire-eater slowly down the Confederate line, speaking words of encouragement to his troops. "His voice was persuasive, encouraging and compelling," the governor recalled. "It was inviting men to death, but they obeyed it." Personally leading the charge himself, the gallant Johnston succeeded in pushing the Federals back about three-fourths of a mile, through a blossoming peach orchard where countless pink pedals fell like rain over the dead and wounded.

Johnston survived the charge unharmed, although his uniform had been nicked by bullets in a couple of places, and still another bullet had torn the sole off one of his boots. As he sat astride his horse near the peach orchard, watching his troops regroup in preparation for a renewed assault, a bullet suddenly tore into his leg and severed an artery. Bleeding was immediate and profuse. If a doctor had been nearby, he could have applied a proper tourniquet and perhaps stopped the flow of blood. However, Johnston had ordered his personal physician to treat a group of wounded soldiers they had passed earlier that day, and the doctor was nowhere near the general. Private Sam Watkins recalled the scene: "Advancing a little further on, we saw General Albert Sidney Johnson [sic] surrounded by his

Johnston's bleeding was immediate and profuse.

staff and Governor Harris, of Tennessee. We saw some little commotion among those who surrounded him, but we did not know at the time that he was dead. The fact was kept from the troops." The great Southern leader of the West lay dead; some say his hand was still clutching the tin cup he had taken from the Yankee camp that morning.

General Johnston died about 2:30 P.M., and the overall command of the Confederate army fell on the shoulders of Gen. P. G. T. Beauregard, who had established his headquarters on the other end of the battlefield in Sherman's captured tent near Shiloh Church. Beauregard did not share Johnston's strategic vision of taking Pittsburg Landing as soon as possible. He simply concentrated on pushing back the entire Federal line. The Union right and left had been driven back two miles from their original positions. Meanwhile, General Prentiss, with the fragments of his division and parts of two others, continued to stand fast in the center along the sunken road. Grant had ordered Prentiss to "maintain that position at all hazards." That is exactly what the stubborn Illinois lawyer did.

Prentiss's new line had first been tested by Missouri colonel John S. Marmaduke and his Third Confederate States Infantry. Missourians, like Tennesseans, fought on both sides in the war, sometimes finding themselves on opposing sides in the same battles. Marmaduke and his men were soon thrown back by the blazing rifles of the defiant Federal troops. Bullets buzzed through the air like angry hornets, snipping underbrush and smacking into trees. As Confederates maneuvered around both his right and left flanks, Prentiss and his men repulsed charge after charge on their position which came to be known as the "Hornet's Nest."

While Grant worked frantically to establish a new defensive line to the rear at Pittsburg Landing ridge, eighteen thousand Southerners closed in on Prentiss's forty-five hundred men. Beauregard put Gen. Daniel Ruggles in command of the Confederate center, and Ruggles immediately brought up as much artillery as possible to bear upon the Hornet's Nest. He had witnessed a dozen unsuccessful, bloody charges on Prentiss's position, and now he accumulated sixty-two pieces of artillery to pound the "Nest" into smithereens and put an end to it all. In a hellish conflagration of smoke and flame, the two sides blazed away at each other, and masses of Union troops finally began to give way, escaping as best they could outside the rear of Prentiss's horseshoe formation. General William Wallace and many of his men, who had held on with Prentiss for hours in the Hornet's Nest, were shot down while

The Hornet's Nest

retreating through a crossfire of Confederate guns in a valley they called "Hell's Hollow." An hour before sunset at 5:30 P.M., General Prentiss, now nearly surrounded, ordered firing to cease and a white flag to be raised; he surrendered twenty-two hundred survivors. However, their incredible stand had bought valuable time for the main portion of the Federal army.

Grant had patched together a powerful defensive line studded with heavy artillery along the ridge at Pittsburg Landing. General Buell's army was now beginning to arrive with the first steamboat full of troops docking at the landing. Two Federal timberclad gunboats, the *Lexington* and *Tyler*, arrived along the shore and added their powerful artillery to the defense of the new Federal position. One last Confederate assault was launched in an attempt to take the landing before nightfall, but Grant's powerful siege guns and the gunboats' artillery from the river's edge aided in throwing back this last Southern effort of the day. About 7:00 P.M. Gen. Lew Wallace's "lost division," which had spent the better part of the day on the wrong road, finally arrived on the field to further reinforce Grant.

The horrific day had at last ended, but the battle itself was not yet over. River transports continued to carry Buell's troops to Pittsburg Landing; their ship bells and steam-powered paddlewheels could be heard all through the night. There in the darkness, wounded, groaning men called out for water. Some crawled to a pond near the sunken road, known thereafter as "Bloody Pond," where men from both sides quenched their thirst as their wounds turned the water red. It was a cold, rainy night with flashes of lightning that briefly lit up scenes of battlefield horror. The gunboats were ordered to lob shells into the Confederate camps on a regular basis all night long, which they did every fifteen minutes. The deadly missiles plowed the earth and splintered trees, sending their limbs crashing down over the heads of tired Southern troops. It was a miserable, sleepless night as many a young soldier awaited his fate on the morrow.

The following morning, April 7, Grant struck first. Reinforced by three fresh divisions, two under Buell and one under Wallace, the Federals far outnumbered their foes. Thus, the tables were turned on the second day of battle as Grant sent forward forty-five thousand troops, half of them fresh, while Beauregard could oppose them with only about twenty thousand weary troops who were still capable of fighting. Despite their successes on the first day of battle, the Confederates had been unable to properly reorganize their scattered forces overnight. Surprisingly, they were not even

Grant impressed no one in person, but all took notice on the battlefield.

able to form a serious line of battle until Grant's forces had already advanced beyond the locations of the Hornet's Nest and the peach orchard, recovering much of the ground they had lost the day before. But once the Southerners fell into line, they put up a stiff resistance, and again the bloody ground shook with the earthquake of a monumental battle. Frenzied charges followed by equally fierce countercharges swayed the battle lines back and forth across the smoke-shrouded field.

In the early part of the afternoon, Grant was riding from the right of the battle line to the left, and back again, with some of his staff to observe the action. Suddenly they were in the thick of artillery and musket fire and hastily rode out of close range and out of sight. They halted to assess the damage; one staff officer's horse was panting heavily. They examined the poor beast and discovered his bullet wound just before the animal dropped to the ground dead. Then Grant noticed that the metal scabbard of his sword had been nearly broken in two by the graze of a bullet. It was not the first time Grant had a close call on the field of Shiloh. The day before, as the final actions of the day raged, Grant held a staff meeting behind his last line of defense by Pittsburg Landing. Suddenly, a cannonball flew through the meeting area, carrying away the head of an officer near Grant. The South lost her army's commanding officer at Shiloh; the North came very close to suffering the same loss.

By 2:00 P.M., General Beauregard reluctantly admitted it was useless to continue the bloody, uneven struggle. His lines had been pushed back, step by step, by the overwhelming numbers of Grant's troops. To prevent a rout, he ordered a strong rear guard, with artillery support, to be positioned on a ridge west of Shiloh Church to hold off his foe as the main body of his army retreated in an orderly fashion from the field. His withdrawal tactics worked well, primarily because the tired and battered Union troops were in no condition to pursue their opponents. The Confederates began their slow, rain-soaked retreat to the southwest toward Corinth. However, the exhausted Southerners had gone only a short distance, still within striking range of the Union army, when they came to a grinding halt, too worn out to march another step.

There is one more footnote to the violent history of the Battle of Shiloh that warrants attention. As the Confederate retreat continued on the morning of April 8, General Sherman led four brigades of infantry and a detachment of cavalry to verify that the Southerners were in fact clearing out of the region. As the Federals followed in the wake of their foes' retreating column, they aroused the wrath of the Confederates' rear guard commander, Lt. Col. Nathan Bedford Forrest. When Sherman's men began to pick their way through a belt of terrain full of fallen trees, appropriately named Fallen Timbers, Forrest charged down upon the advance skirmishers and sent them flying. With only 350 cavalry troopers, Forrest continued his charge right into the main Federal line of two thousand rifles. His cavalrymen wisely drew in the reins of their mounts at the sight of the bristling line, but their leader continued his mad dash, plunging right into the midst of his foes, slashing away with his saber in a war-crazed frenzy. Suddenly realizing he was alone, Forrest whirled his horse around and proceeded to cut his way out. At that moment, a Yank jammed the barrel of his rifle into Forrest's side and squeezed the trigger. The force of the resulting blast literally lifted the fierce cavalry officer out of his saddle as a bullet tore into his body and lodged against his spine. But Forrest was no ordinary mortal man; he immediately regained his balance in the saddle, grabbed an infantryman by the collar, and with an iron grip, lifted him onto his horse's rump. Holding the terrified soldier as a human shield, he galloped away. As Forrest neared the safety of his own line, he flung his captive to the ground and proceeded to begin his rapid recovery from a wound that would have ended the military career of most men. Thus, the astounding Rebel warrior, who was already turning himself into a legend, became the last man wounded in the Shiloh conflict.

The huge battle appalled the citizens of both North and

Forrest boldly rode into the Union line . . .

South once they saw the casualty lists. Shiloh was the largest
battle of any war America had ever endured up to that time.
Grant had approximately 65,000 troops involved in the battle,
counting his reinforcements from Buell. His losses were 1,754
killed, 8,408 wounded, and 2,885 captured or missing; a total
of 13,047 casualties. Johnston and Beauregard had about
44,000 troops to fight the great battle. They lost 1,728 killed,
8,012 wounded, and 959 captured or missing; a total of 10,699

. . . realized he was alone and wheeled his horse to leave, but not before one soldier fired point blank . . .

casualties. Those who believed the war would be short and relatively light in bloodshed awoke to reality after Shiloh. Americans were shocked and outraged at the carnage. Both sides now realized it would be a long, hard, bloody conflict that would leave no family untouched by tragedy. The horrific battle in Tennessee had proved that both Yankee and Rebel were tough, stubborn fighters and that there would be no easy conclusion to the "Great Rebellion."

The same day that Beauregard left the gory field at Shiloh, a nearly bloodless, but significant, Federal victory was won just off the northwestern tip of Tennessee on the mighty Mississippi River. The story began after the fall of Fort Henry, when the Confederates evacuated their stronghold at Columbus, Kentucky, and moved men, artillery, and supplies

. . . Forrest was still able to snatch a private by the collar and . . .

down the Mississippi to Island Number 10, so called because it was the tenth island downstream from Cairo. This two-mile piece of high ground was transformed into a Southern stronghold that blocked Northern shipping on the great river. Seven thousand troops, more than fifty heavy artillery pieces, and numerous smaller field guns made the island a Confederate Gibraltar. In response, General Halleck ordered Foote's river fleet to shell the island's batteries while the newly formed Army of the Mississippi (not to be confused with the Confederate version), under Brig. Gen. John Pope, closed in by land from the Missouri side of the river. This strategy eventually cut off Island Number 10's garrison from three sides, leaving only the swampy Tennessee bank of the river open for supplies to get through to the besieged Confederates. Under the cover of two

. . . make his escape using the lad as a human shield.

ironclads' artillery, Pope at last succeeded in getting troops across to the Tennessee side and completely cutting off the Southern garrison from supplies.

A small squadron of Confederate Navy vessels did the best they could to defend the island. Benjamin F. Hughes recalled his service on one such vessel, which was a poor match for the

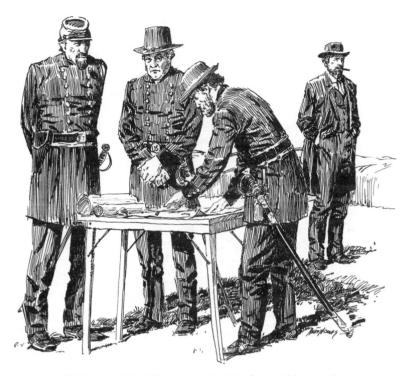

Halleck considered Grant a rival and a threat to his authority.

Union ironclads: "I was ordered to the 'Manassas' which had arrived from New Orleans and I went to duty as Master of that vessel with Cpt. Wesley commanding and in time the Island of Number Ten and Madrid bend was besieged and bombarded and we took our post and kept up the cannonading for some time each day fighting until finaly [sic] we had to abandon it and go to New Orleans preparatory for the battle that was to be at the mouth of the river. . . ." Finally surrounded, the powerful island fortress surrendered on April 7. Thus, eighty miles of the upper Mississippi River passed into Federal control with the loss of less than one hundred men on both sides.

After taking Island Number 10, Pope and his army were

ordered to join Grant and Buell at Pittsburg Landing where Halleck planned to take personal command of the combined armies, numbering more than a hundred thousand men, and lead an advance on Corinth, Mississippi. Arriving at Pittsburg Landing on April 11, Halleck once again revealed his distrust in Grant by removing him from field command and basically putting him on a shelf by appointing him to a meaningless post as second in command of the combined forces. A depressed Grant requested a transfer, but then, after words of encouragement from Sherman, he chose to stay on and wait it out. Sherman recalled their conversation: "I argued with him that, if he went away events would go right along, and he would be left out. Whereas, if he remained some happy accident might restore him to favor and his true place."

After meticulous preparations, Halleck began a creeping advance on Corinth, twenty-two miles southwest of Pittsburg Landing. The overly cautious, paranoid general advanced less than one mile a day and ordered his troops to construct detailed breastworks each night to prevent another Shiloh-style surprise attack. The huge, lumbering Federal force finally arrived on the outskirts of Corinth on May 28, and the next day, they began bombarding the Confederate defenses. Beauregard, vastly outnumbered, chose to retreat fifty miles farther south to Tupelo. However, in an effort to escape with an extra margin of safety, he concocted a clever deception. Beauregard ordered train locomotives to chug in and out of town regularly to the accompaniment of loud cheering by his troops in order to convince the Federals he was receiving ample reinforcements. The ruse worked, and "Old Brains" Halleck was afraid to advance until his troops could hear the explosions from the Confederate rear guard blowing up supplies that couldn't be evacuated. On May 30, the huge Federal force marched triumphantly into Corinth.

The loss of Corinth, a vital link on the Memphis and Charleston Railroad, was a heavy blow to the Confederacy. As a result, Jefferson Davis soon replaced Beauregard with dour

Maj. Gen. Braxton Bragg, who would earn the dubious distinction of personally being responsible for killing more Confederates than Federals by his liberal use of the firing squad as punishment. To further lower Southern morale, the Confederate government had instituted the draft on April 16. Private Sam Watkins expressed the feelings of many Southern troops: "From this time on till the end of the war, a soldier was simply a machine, a conscript. It was mighty rough on rebels. We cursed the war, we cursed Bragg, we cursed the Southern Confederacy. All our pride and valor had gone, and we were sick of war and the Southern Confederacy."

The eyes of the Federal high command now fell upon the Confederacy's fifth largest city, Memphis, Tennessee. Before the fall of Corinth, the river route to Memphis had been blocked by Fort Pillow, fifty miles upstream. After Corinth fell, Beauregard ordered Fort Pillow evacuated as he established a new line of defense farther south. It was a pity to simply walk away from the Tennessee post after it had witnessed a very dramatic Confederate naval action in its defense on May 10. A U.S. Navy flotilla was bombarding Fort Pillow when eight Confederate gunboats, some with light armor and others completely unarmored, came around a bend in the river called Plum Point. The Confederate River Defense Fleet under the command of Commodore James E. Montgomery, was a poor match for the fleet of U.S. ironclads under Capt. Charles Davis. However, the Rebel vessels had been converted into "rams" with iron prows designed to smash into an enemy craft and punch a gaping hole below its waterline. As the Confederate gunboats came into full view of the Union flotilla, the rams CSS *Bragg* and *Sterling Price* sped toward the USS *Cincinnati* (a veteran of the battle for Fort Henry) and slammed into its hull. The *Cincinnati* turned in the river, only to be rammed again by the *Sumter.* Then the *Cincinnati*'s captain came on deck to get a better view and was immediately shot down by a Confederate sharpshooter. The Federal ship soon sank in the muddy Mississippi water. The USS *Mound City* and *Carondelet* (a veteran of Fort Henry, Fort Donelson, and Island Number 10) joined the battle, but soon after, a well-placed artillery shell from the *Van Dorn* tore a four-foot gash in the *Mound City,* which managed to near the shore before it sank in the shallows. As the *Pittsburgh* (a veteran of Fort Donelson) and *Benton* neared the battle area, Commodore Montgomery signaled his ships to retire toward Fort Pillow. The Federal fleet chased the lighter, faster Confederate vessels until they came within range of Fort Pillow's guns. The post's artillery thundered a greeting to the U.S. ships, which promptly broke off their pursuit. For the remainder of the month, the two little fleets continued to play a game of cat and mouse with the guns of Fort Pillow joining the action whenever the Federals came within range. But on June 4, steamboats helped evacuate the fort's defenders as the troops and gunboats retired downriver by order of Beauregard. Memphis itself would be the next objective of the Federals.

Captain Davis's little fleet had been reinforced by a flotilla of Federal rams on May 25. Four civilian steamboats had been outfitted for war and converted to rams by Col. Charles Ellet Jr., a brilliant fifty-seven-year-old engineer with a fierce dedication to the Union Cause. He had advocated the use of rams by the U.S. Navy long before the Confederates proved how effective they could be. However, the navy was unimpressed, so he took his case to Secretary of War Edwin Stanton. Stanton was impressed, commissioned Ellet a colonel, and authorized him to build a ram fleet under the authority of the U.S. Army. Ellet was given personal command of the fleet he created. He chose his brother, Lt. Col. Alfred W. Ellet, as his second-in-command. Among his junior officers were his son, Charles Rivers Ellet, and his nephews, Edward, Richard, and John Ellet. Colonel Ellet signed up riverboat men rather than naval personnel for his crews.

On June 6, Ellet and his four rams, accompanied by five of Captain Davis's ironclads, chugged downriver toward Memphis. Confederate commodore James Montgomery

The General Price *was rammed as the* Beauregard *suddenly exploded.*

prepared to defend the city with his eight light gunboat rams. Word spread through the city like wildfire that the Federal fleet was approaching, and crowds of citizens headed for the river landing to watch the deadly drama of a naval battle. Soon there were thousands of excited spectators lining the bluffs above the river to cheer on Montgomery's vessels as they boldly maneuvered to attack the oncoming Federal fleet which had just come into view.

Colonel Ellet led the Federal approach on board the USS *Queen of the West.* He rammed the lead Confederate vessel, CSS *General Lovell,* at a speed of fifteen knots. The shock of the great collision could be felt on the bluffs as river water rushed through a huge, gaping hole in the bow of the *Lovell.* The Rebel gunboat soon disappeared beneath the muddy river water. The colonel's brother Alfred's ship, *Monarch,* swiftly squeezed between two Confederate rams converging on him, the *General Beauregard* and *Sterling Price.* As a result, the two Southern vessels collided with each other. Alfred then circled back and rammed the *Price,* which ran aground. Meanwhile, the *Beauregard,* damaged from the collision and riddled by Federal shells, suddenly exploded with a mighty roar as her boilers burst. The spectators on shore were horrified by these developments and boisterously yelled their disapproval like sports fans at a ballpark. Among them, standing next to his horse, was a Missouri officer in charge of the small Confederate land force assigned to defend Memphis, Brig. Gen. M. Jeff Thompson. As the crowd cheered their fleet on, Thompson impassively watched the action, knowing the fate of Memphis was being decided on the great body of muddy water before him and that he was powerless to offer assistance. Meanwhile, Captain Davis's ironclads had gotten into the thick of the action. Thunderous salvos from their powerful guns sank another Confederate vessel and disabled three others. Brave Commodore Montgomery was killed in action aboard his flagship, the *Little Rebel.*

The citizens of Memphis were mortified. They had turned out to cheer their fleet on to victory only to see their "home team" utterly defeated with the fleet destroyed and their land force immediately preparing to retreat. General Thompson, after watching the devastation of the Confederate flotilla, tersely snapped, "They are gone, and I am going." Then he galloped away from the scene. Charles R. Ellet, the nineteen-year-old son of Colonel Ellet (who was wounded in the leg during the action), led a four-man detachment ashore to raise the Stars and Stripes over the Memphis post office and claim the city for the Federal Union. Governor Harris and his Confederate state government were once again forced to move, becoming a wandering government in exile. As for Colonel Ellet, his wound became infected, and the brave Union patriot died two weeks after taking Memphis. His son Charles was promoted, becoming the youngest colonel in the U.S. Army, and was given command of the ram fleet. Captain Charles Davis, in the meantime, took his U.S. naval squadron downriver after securing the Mississippi along Tennessee's shores and awaited further orders a few miles upstream from the city of Vicksburg, Mississippi. Thus, the war for the Mississippi River along Tennessee's waterfront came to an end.

After the Federal capture of Corinth, General Halleck had sent Brigadier General Buell and his Army of the Ohio eastward to attempt to take Chattanooga, Tennessee, one of the Confederacy's most important railroad junctions. The man assigned to hold Chattanooga for the Confederacy was Maj. Gen. Edmund Kirby Smith who had an army of six small brigades known as the Army of East Tennessee. His force was also supposed to hold the East Tennessee and Georgia Railroad between Chattanooga and the Cumberland Gap, a distance of 180 miles. Smith of course, requested reinforcements. He was a West Point graduate and professional soldier who had also been a mathematics professor at the Point before the war. He was a Confederate hero of the first Battle of Manassas, where he was wounded. Smith chose to disrupt Buell's advance by sending two of his best cavalry commanders on raids. Colonel Nathan B. Forrest took Murfreesboro on July 13 (capturing twelve hundred prisoners) and cut the railroad behind Buell's advance. Soon after, Col. John Hunt Morgan, after completing a very successful raid through Kentucky, destroyed the vital railroad tunnel at Gallatin, Tennessee. It was an eight-hundred-foot tunnel that had been cut through a mountain north of town. Morgan's men set fire to captured railroad cars loaded with hay and pushed them into the tunnel. The timber supports caught fire and burned until the tunnel collapsed. Since utilizing the railroad system was vital to Buell's plan, his advance came to a grinding halt.

Meanwhile General Bragg began moving thirty-four thousand troops from Tupelo to Chattanooga, leaving thirty-two thousand men to defend central Mississippi. In the largest Confederate railroad movement of the war, he sent his infantry divisions on a 776-mile rail journey south to Mobile, northeast to Atlanta, and then north to Chattanooga. Thus he flanked Buell's force by rail and made military history in one of the first significant military maneuvers utilizing the railroad. By mid-August, Bragg with his Army of the Mississippi and Smith with his Army of East Tennessee were ready to march north in a bold invasion of Kentucky. The invasion plan, mainly devised by Smith, was intended to draw Buell's army back north, out of Tennessee, and possibly even secure the state of Kentucky for the Confederacy. Bragg and Smith had high hopes of recruiting large numbers of Confederate sympathizers in Kentucky once they arrived.

As the great armies marched north and vied to outmaneuver each other in Kentucky, the war continued in Tennessee. Small forces still carried on the fight for control of the state. Those who died in the resulting half-forgotten skirmishes sacrificed just as much as those who perished in the huge, famous battles. One small force was particularly interesting due to its membership: the Confederate Legion of Cherokee Indians and Highlanders, better known as simply the "Thomas Legion" after its commander, Col. William H. Thomas. The Eastern Band of Cherokee, as they came to be known, was a small branch of the tribe that had escaped the Removal of 1838 (the dreadful "Trail of Tears") and remained in their homeland of western North Carolina. When war came in 1861, about four hundred Cherokee men followed their colorful leader, William H. Thomas (whose Indian name was Wil-Usdi), into Confederate service. Thomas was a white man who had been adopted into the tribe at the age of twelve by the Cherokees' chief. He had become a highly successful businessman and politician but never forgot his Cherokee family and friends and became the band's staunch defender on legal and civic matters before the war. A strong advocate of states' rights, Thomas sided with the Confederacy and raised a unit of Indian and white troops with infantry, cavalry, and artillery branches. By mid-July of 1862, his force had grown to battalion size with two full companies of Cherokee troops and six companies of white soldiers. The Legion's first serious clash with Federal troops occurred at Baptist Gap near Rogersville, Tennessee, on

*Cherokees of the Thomas Legion fought for the South in the
Great Smoky Mountains.*

September 13-15, 1862. The skirmish took place when Union
forces attempted to pass through a gap south of the
Cumberland Mountains and enter eastern Tennessee.
Cherokees of the Thomas Legion routed the Yanks and drove
them from the region. Several of the fallen Union troops were
found to be scalped, which resulted in a storm of protest in the
Northern newspapers. The Federal military governor, Andrew
Johnson, publicly denounced the scalpings and took advantage of the incident for war propaganda purposes. Operating
primarily in the Great Smoky Mountain region of eastern
Tennessee and western North Carolina, the Thomas Legion

continued to serve the Confederate cause throughout the war, blocking Union incursions through the Smokies, serving as sentinels in the mountain passes, opposing Union partisans and recruiters, and helping to enforce the unpopular Confederate Conscription Act in the region.

Meanwhile in Kentucky, the Confederate invasion did not meet with the success General Bragg had hoped for. Few new recruits volunteered to serve in his ragged, half-starved army, and as he tried to outmaneuver Buell and his army, Bragg wound up with his forces scattered over a sixty-mile front when the big showdown finally occurred. As a result, Bragg had to fight the Battle of Perryville with only sixteen thousand troops, while his opponent, Buell, had more than thirty-nine thousand soldiers present. Fortunately for Bragg, Buell only committed about twenty-two thousand into the battle on October 8, thinking he would need fresh troops for the following day's action. The combat at Perryville was horrific. Private Sam Watkins, serving in Bragg's army, described the scenes: "Such obstinate fighting I never had seen before or since. The guns were discharged so rapidly that it seemed the earth itself was in a volcanic uproar. The iron storm passed through our ranks, mangling and tearing men to pieces. The very air seemed full of stifling smoke and fire which seemed the very pit of hell, peopled by contending demons." By the end of the action, forty-two hundred Federals and thirty-four hundred Confederates had become casualties. Bragg had tactically come out ahead of Buell in the bloody contest, but the Southern commander was aware of how greatly outnumbered he was and dared not risk another day of battle at Perryville.

Thus, the Confederates retreated during the night, and for the next few days the contending forces maneuvered cautiously. Outnumbered and short on supplies, Bragg became intensely pessimistic and suddenly chose to abandon his Kentucky campaign. Bragg and Smith marched their forces back into Tennessee, and the Federal government's grip on Kentucky remained firm for the rest of the war. Eventually,

William Starke Rosecrans

Bragg set up his headquarters at Murfreesboro. As for Buell, he had slowly followed the retreating Confederates as far as Nashville, where he firmly planted himself at Federal headquarters. Telegrams from Washington failed to prod him into further action, and Lincoln replaced the overcautious commander with Maj. Gen. William S. Rosecrans, and the Army of the Ohio was officially renamed Army of the Cumberland.

General Bragg fell under a storm of criticism for his failure in the Kentucky campaign and had to travel to Richmond to explain his actions to President Davis. Davis, Bragg's old Mexican War buddy, was satisfied with the cantankerous general's explanation and retained him in his position. However, he assigned Gen. Joseph E. Johnston to overall command of the Western Theater, including Bragg and his forces, and renamed the Army of the Mississippi, the Army of Tennessee.

Murfreesboro was a serene setting for the Army of Tennessee's winter camp. It was nearly unscarred by the war in

Morgan's men endured the freezing march to Hartsville.

the late autumn of 1862 as Bragg's troops settled in for a much-needed rest. The idyllic Southern town welcomed her brave boys in gray with open arms, and many civilian kitchens worked overtime preparing home-cooked meals for the hungry soldiers. The women of the community also sewed numerous uniforms to replace the tattered rags worn by many of the men. The officers enjoyed attending social events in the mild weather that set in around Murfreesboro. The troops even had a little victory to celebrate in early December thanks to dashing Col. John Hunt Morgan.

Morgan was assigned by Bragg to raid the Federal supply lines to Nashville. The Kentucky colonel chose to meet the challenge head-on by attacking one of the main Union bases guarding the railroad line from Louisville to Nashville. The

Federal camp at Hartsville was thirty-five miles northeast of Nashville and was home to an entire brigade of Union troops. On December 6, Morgan set out for Hartsville at the head of a mixed force of cavalry, infantry, and artillery. The weather had become frosty, and crossing the Cumberland River turned into a bitter ordeal for those cavalrymen who had to ride their swimming horses through the ice-cold water. Morgan's infantry detachment had to take turns utilizing only two boats at a ferry crossing. Once they finally reached the perimeter of Hartsville on December 7, the element of surprise was lost as Federal pickets alerted the entire camp of the Confederates' advance. Nevertheless, Morgan's tactics were effective as dismounted cavalry hit the right of the Federal line, and Kentucky infantrymen struck the left. Meanwhile Morgan's howitzers, across the river on the south bank of the Cumberland, began blasting away at the camp, drawing the Yanks' artillery fire away from the defense of their flanks. The Federals were soon "crowded together like sheep in a pen, and were falling fast," as one of Morgan's officers, Col. Basil Duke, wrote. "The white flag was hoisted in an hour and a half after the first shot had been fired." Morgan and his men returned to Murfreesboro with 1,834 Union prisoners and a stunning little victory under their belts to lift Confederate morale.

Southern partisan activity against Rosecran's Army of the Cumberland increased around the region of Nashville where the Federal troops were encamped. In a dramatic masquerade, Confederate guerrillas wearing Federal overcoats burned five steamboats being utilized by the Union army on the Cumberland River in early December. However, the most notorious incident of partisan activity in the region during this time period was an attack on a passenger train of the Nashville and Louisville Railroad. Guerrillas derailed the train, sending the engine and front cars off the track. They then opened fire on the wreck with small arms. In retaliation, the Federals made a sweep of the countryside north of Nashville and hanged a number of suspected guerrillas.

Meanwhile, Bragg's Army of Tennessee had a distinguished visitor in camp. None other than Pres. Jefferson Davis himself arrived at Murfreesboro on December 10 to inspect the troops. He stayed for two days. Davis reviewed the army, met with officers, was serenaded by the army band, and gave a speech to a crowd gathered in front of his hotel. He also rewarded Morgan for his Hartsville raid with a commission as brigadier general. However, Davis's visit was not merely a goodwill tour. He wanted to see firsthand if Bragg's army was strong enough to spare men with which he could reinforce Vicksburg, Mississippi, which was being threatened by General Grant. The new commander of the Confederate Western Theater, Gen. Joseph Johnston, had earlier objected to the plan, stating that it would seriously weaken the Army of Tennessee which needed its full strength to counter Rosecran's Army of the Cumberland. But Davis saw nothing on this trip to change his mind and ordered a division of about nine thousand troops of the Army of Tennessee (one-fourth of Bragg's infantry) to be sent to

Vicksburg. Bragg protested that this move would leave him with fewer than forty thousand men to oppose Rosecrans, whose force had been estimated at sixty-five thousand at Nashville alone. Yet Davis's mind was made up. He did not hesitate to overrule his generals because he considered himself to be just as good a military strategist as any of them, if not better. He was a West Point graduate and had served with distinction in the Mexican War. He had also been an excellent U.S. secretary of war. As a matter of fact, Davis would have preferred to serve as a general in the current conflict but had bowed to the will of the people and grudgingly accepted the presidency. Thus, Bragg lost a large portion of his army before he and Rosecrans had even met in battle. Davis advised Bragg: "Fight if you can and fall back beyond the Tennessee." Unknown to either Bragg or Davis, it would be necessary to "fight if you can" much sooner than either anticipated.

General Rosecrans had no intention of sitting in camp at Nashville all winter long. Not content, like Bragg, to wait till spring for a new campaign, Rosecrans had immediately begun logistical preparations to march on Murfreesboro. He called a council of war on Christmas night. As his officers sipped cups of yuletide spirits, Rosecrans outlined his final plans and issued orders to march in the morning.

By December 27, the Army of the Cumberland was encountering stiff resistance by hard-riding detachments of Confederate cavalry. Although Bragg had sent both General Morgan and Colonel Forrest away on raids, he did retain a force of cavalry in the region of Murfreesboro under a young, energetic officer, Brig. Gen. Joseph Wheeler. "Fighting Joe," as he was called, gave the advancing Federals a hard time in several skirmishes. Wheeler's richest prize in his series of raids on Rosecrans's advancing forces was near the town of LaVergne, where he captured a Federal supply train of three hundred wagons. He took seven hundred prisoners and destroyed nearly a million dollars worth of U.S. government supplies, looting and burning the huge wagon train. Fighting Joe harassed and

delayed the Union advance long enough for Bragg to consolidate his forces and prepare for the massive onslaught of
Federal military power.

By December 30, the Army of the Cumberland faced the
Army of Tennessee drawn up for battle along the banks of
Stones River on the western outskirts of Murfreesboro. By
coincidence, the opposing commanders formulated essential-
ly the same battle plan for the following day: both planned to
launch an assault on their foe's right wing. Bragg had approximately 37,700 troops, and Rosecrans had about 43,300.
Fortunately for the Confederates, almost half of the 82,000-
man Army of the Cumberland was occupied guarding the vital
railroad (supply line) from Louisville, and many also remained
in garrison at Nashville to insure the Federal grip on the state
capital. As the two hostile armies camped for the night only a
few hundred yards from each other, their military bands began
a musical duel. The Federal musicians played patriotic U.S.
tunes such as "Yankee Doodle," while the Confederate musicians replied with "Dixie" and other Southern favorites.
Finally, one band played a haunting rendition of "Home Sweet
Home." Musicians on both sides picked up the tune as thousands of troops wearing blue and gray began to sing the words
in unison. The next day, they would commence shooting at
each other.

Early on the morning of December 31, the Confederates
struck first with a hard-fisted assault that drove the Union right
and part of the center back to the road to Nashville known as
the Nashville Turnpike. Only tenacious fighting by Federal
troops led by two stubborn generals, George H. Thomas (the
victor of Mill Springs, Kentucky, in 1861) and Philip H.
Sheridan (a tough little scrapper who was rapidly making a
name for himself), kept the Union army from a complete rout.
Confederate infantryman Sam Watkins, wounded in the arm,
recalled seeing his heroic division commander, Maj. Gen.
Benjamin F. Cheatham of Tennessee, rally his troops for another charge: "I saw either victory or death written on his face. He

A haunting rendition of "Home Sweet Home"

was leading the charge in person. Then it was that I saw the power of one man, born to command, over a multitude of men then almost routed and demoralized. I saw and felt that he was not fighting for glory, but that he was fighting for his country because he loved that country, and he was willing to give his life for his country and the success of our cause."

Rosecrans rushed fresh Union troops to his new defensive line on high ground near the Nashville Turnpike and the tracks of the Nashville and Chattanooga Railroad located on an embankment. Bragg's men emerged from the trees and charged Rosecrans's new position only to be hit hard by a devastating storm of lead. Charge after charge failed to break the Union line as desperate hand-to-hand combat ensued to no avail. Finally, Bragg's exhausted infantrymen were ordered to fall back as the fighting fizzled out. During the day's blazing action, General Rosecrans himself experienced a close call frighteningly similar to the incident that befell Grant at Shiloh. While he was riding with his staff close to the front lines, a cannonball decapitated his chief of staff right next to him, splattering blood across his uniform.

The Army of Tennessee had been victorious in the overall measure of the day's events, driving the Federals back for miles in a pell-mell retreat that nearly turned into a rout that bloody morning. As darkness fell over the cold, smoky battlefield, General Bragg wired Richmond of a great victory and settled in for a New Year's Eve rest, expecting Rosecrans and his Army of the Cumberland to retreat in the morning.

CHAPTER 3

By Force of Arms: 1863

New Year's Day 1863 dawned with gray winter clouds spitting sleet and rain down upon the battlefield near Murfreesboro. Rosecrans had not retreated; his troops stubbornly held their position on the field. Bragg glared through his field glasses at the Federal line, contemptuously watching units march to new positions and wondering if "Old Rosy" planned to retreat or renew the battle. All day long the two sides shifted men, ordnance, and equipment, warily watching each other as the popping and cracking sounds of sharpshooters' rifles broke the crisp, cold air. A few skirmishes took place, but the most important troop movement occurred after dark when a Union division crossed the ice-cold waters of Stones River and took position on a ridge that commanded the Confederate right.

January 2 began as the previous day, with sleet falling incessantly and each side stubbornly waiting for the other to retreat or attack. At last an artillery duel commenced, and both sides probed each other's positions, but no decisive action occurred until the afternoon. Bragg ordered an attack to take the ridge dominating the right of his line, occupied by a Union division the night before. Major General John C. Breckinridge was summoned to Bragg's headquarters and ordered to make the assault with his division of Kentucky and Tennessee infantry.

Breckinridge protested the decision, pointing out the folly of what he believed to be a suicidal assault because Union artillery on high ground across the river would enfilade his line. Bragg refused to rescind his order, and Breckinridge continued to protest almost to the point of insubordination. Finally, an angry Bragg silenced his subordinate, warning him that he expected the order to be obeyed. Breckinridge, a loyal soldier devoted to the Southern Cause, prepared to do his duty. He had been vice president of the United States and the Southern Democrats' candidate for president, opposing Lincoln in the election of 1860. He most likely would have been a better choice for president of the Confederacy than Jefferson Davis. Nevertheless, the tall, brave Kentucky gentleman was now a division commander under General Bragg, and he had to carry out his orders as a good soldier should.

When Breckinridge informed his brigade and regimental commanders of Bragg's order, they nearly mutinied. The Kentucky troops especially hated Bragg because he seemed to look down on them, perhaps because Kentucky men did not flock to enlist during Bragg's ill-fated campaign through their state. One of Bragg's most recent firing squad executions had even been inflicted upon a popular member of the First Kentucky Brigade. This brigade, under fiery Brig. Gen. Roger W. Hanson, was famed for its fighting ability, devotion to the Confederacy, and fondness for whiskey. The "Orphan Brigade," as the unit came to be known because its native state of Kentucky was in enemy hands, had proved its courage well at Shiloh. General Hanson fumed at the order to send his men into a death trap. He believed Bragg had deliberately issued a murderous order, and he actually proposed to personally go to Bragg's headquarters and kill him! However, Breckinridge, the obedient soldier and respected leader, finally quieted his officers down and brought order to the tense situation. He set to work deploying his division of forty-five hundred troops with Hanson's Kentucky "Orphans" on the left of the battle line and a brigade of Tennessee infantry on the right under Brig. Gen.

Gideon J. Pillow, formerly second-in-command at Fort Donelson. In support, two hundred yards to the rear, were two more brigades.

The stage was set for one of the most dramatic charges of the war as Breckinridge's division stood in a half-mile long battle line on the east side of Stones River. Before them was six hundred yards of open ground they had to cross to get to the ridge which they had to seize from a full division of Federal troops backed up by artillery from across the river. At 4:00 P.M. the long gray line surged forward as Confederate artillery on high ground to the rear roared in support of the grand assault. The Rebel yell pierced the chilly winter air as Union artillery shells began to scream through the air, tearing and plowing through the ranks and exploding in thunderclap balls of fire and smoke. In thirty minutes of nightmare carnage, Breckinridge's men had done the impossible—they had taken the ridge and were pursuing the routed Yanks over the crest. But the worst was yet to come for the dauntless young men in gray: as they poured over the crest of the ridge, fifty-eight artillery pieces across the river unleashed another horrific cannonade into their ranks. Shells slammed into the Confederate force at the unbearable rate of a hundred rounds per minute. Then massed Union infantry crossed Stones River in a furious counterattack. Breckinridge's troops were driven back to their starting point, having lost fifteen hundred men in one hour. Among the mortally wounded was Gen. Roger Hanson of the Orphan Brigade.

Darkness soon fell on the morbid landscape of the battlefield. During the night Bragg continued to receive disheartening casualty reports, and Wheeler's cavalry reported Federal reinforcements arriving from Nashville. By the morning of January 3, Bragg was aware of his sad state of affairs. Nearly a quarter of his force had been killed or wounded, his foe was being reinforced, and his corps commanders, Hardee and Polk, both recommended retreat. That afternoon, the Confederate withdrawal began, and by nightfall, the Army of

Artillery shells tore through the ranks of the Orphan Brigade.

Tennessee was in full retreat to a new position behind the Duck River near Tullahoma, twenty-five miles to the south. The battle had cost the Confederates 1,236 killed, 7,766 wounded, and 868 captured or missing. Federal casualties were 1,630 killed, 7,397 wounded, 3,673 captured or missing. The Federals now set their sights on Chattanooga, gateway to the Deep South. But stubborn old Bragg would not give way without more fighting, and the Army of the Cumberland was so crippled by its costly victory near Murfreesboro that Rosecrans would not renew his offensive for several months. Nevertheless, news of victory at Stones River brought a bit of cheer to the North and greatly relieved Lincoln whose administration was under severe criticism and pressure since a disastrous Federal defeat at Fredericksburg, Virginia, on December 13. The president wired Rosecrans a congratulatory message which included a very emotional statement: "I can never forget, whilst I remember anything, you gave us a hard earned victory which, had there been defeat instead, the nation could hardly have lived over."

For six months, the Army of the Cumberland regrouped and built up its strength in and around Murfreesboro, while Washington, D. C., impatiently urged General Rosecrans to take the offensive once again. Meanwhile, the Army of Tennessee fortified a line along Duck River near Tullahoma, barring the Federals' route to Chattanooga. The little Tennessee city of just over twenty-five hundred residents was destined to play a key role in the war. Holding Chattanooga was vital to the Confederacy; it was the terminus of major railroads leading northeast to Knoxville and Richmond, southeast to Atlanta, and northwest to Nashville and Louisville.

On June 24, Rosecrans finally took the offensive as the Army of the Cumberland broke camp and marched south. At Stones River he had proved he was a tough fighter; now in a ten-day-long series of marches and skirmishing known as the Tullahoma Campaign, Old Rosy would prove himself capable of brilliant strategy. In a sort of fencing match with Bragg,

Rosecrans executed flanking movements and indirect marches of troop columns that in effect, feinted Bragg out of Tennessee's heartland. Some tough skirmishing did take place in mountain passes: Hoover's and Liberty Gaps. Action was especially hot at Liberty Gap where the Federal advance was delayed by troops led by Maj. Gen. Patrick R. Cleburne, who had established a shining reputation as one of the best generals in the Western Theater by his gallant actions at Shiloh and Stones River. Cleburne was an Irish immigrant who had served in the British Army. His name was becoming well known to his foes, and he earned the nickname of the "Stonewall Jackson of the West." However, tough combat by the Federals, especially Wilder's Brigade, a unit of mounted infantry armed with seven-shot Spencer repeating rifles (led by Col. John T. Wilder), broke through the mountain gaps. Soon the Federal army had outmaneuvered General Bragg's Duck River defenses. The Confederate army fell back across the Tennessee River to Chattanooga itself. President Davis's words from the past December (when he took away a fourth of the army's infantry) must have echoed in Bragg's mind: "Fight if you can and fall back beyond the Tennessee."

Rosecrans arrived in Tullahoma on July 3. His campaign had been a model of planning and execution; the Confederates had been nearly swept from Tennessee at a cost of 84 Federal dead and 476 wounded (Southern losses were never reported). However, the Tullahoma Campaign received scant attention in the newspapers and Washington because of the two monumental Federal triumphs that occurred during the same remarkable time period. On July 4, Gen. Robert E. Lee's Army of Northern Virginia retreated back toward its home state after a crushing defeat at Gettysburg, Pennsylvania. On that same day in Vicksburg, Mississippi, General Grant accepted the surrender of that great Southern stronghold, opening the Mississippi to Federal control and splitting the Confederacy in two. By July 7, General Rosecrans was receiving telegrams from Washington urging him to renew his offensive operations with no congratulatory message for his recent Tullahoma triumph.

Much to the frustration of Washington, it was not until August 16 when Old Rosy finally began his complex movement to Chattanooga. He hoped to repeat the success of his maneuvers in the Tullahoma Campaign, outflanking his foe and taking his objective with minimal casualties. Once again columns of troops entered narrow mountain passes, each unit coordinating its movements as best it could with other units advancing south. General Bragg, nervously entrenched at Chattanooga with an army plagued by illness and desertions, had only about thirty thousand men fit for service. He received reports of Federal advances that seemed to be coming from all over his map. Frustrated, he expressed his anxiety to Lt. Gen. Daniel Harvey Hill who had been transferred from the Eastern Theater to replace corps commander General Hardee who was sent to Mississippi to aid General Johnston. Bragg stated, "It is said to be easy to defend a mountainous country, but mountains hide your foe from you, while they are full of gaps through which he can pounce on you at any time."

Bragg repeatedly wired Richmond for reinforcements as the Army of the Cumberland cautiously closed in on Chattanooga. Meanwhile, to the northeast, a twenty-four-thousand-man Union force called the Army of the Ohio (not to be confused with the previous Army of the Ohio which became the Army of the Cumberland) closed in on Knoxville held by Maj. Gen. Simon B. Buckner who had only about eight thousand troops to hold East Tennessee for the Confederacy. After his surrender at Fort Donelson, Buckner was a prisoner of war until released in a prisoner exchange. Now he once again found himself in a humiliating situation, having to evacuate Knoxville before he was overrun by overwhelming numbers of Federal troops. The luckless general marched his force to Chattanooga to reinforce Bragg, while on September 2, Maj. Gen. Ambrose E. Burnside's Army of the Ohio entered Knoxville. Union sympathizers in and around the town welcomed the blue-coated troops with open arms.

By now, Federals outside of Chattanooga were occasionally lobbing artillery shells into the town as their comrades in other units marched in through the mountain passes. On September 1, "Fighting Joe" Wheeler's cavalry patrols confirmed the report that a powerful Union force was pouring into the mountains south of Chattanooga. Yet Bragg dared not march large numbers of his troops away from the northern approaches to the city since he believed the main Union assault would come from that direction. For a week, Bragg's staff struggled with incoming reports of Federal advances and tried to figure out which ones to believe. On three separate occasions Bragg started to pull out of Chattanooga but then changed his mind. Finally, the Army of Tennessee's perilous situation became obvious: Rosecrans had indeed outflanked the Southerners, crossed the Tennessee River well below Chattanooga, and had large numbers of troops in the rear of Bragg's defenses.

On September 7, Bragg evacuated Chattanooga. Thus, the Gateway to the Deep South fell into Federal hands without a battle. Rosecrans had once again achieved a tremendous victory through masterful military maneuvering rather than savage bloodletting. Yet the Army of Tennessee was still a force to be reckoned with, especially since Richmond had at last responded to Bragg's appeals for reinforcements. The Confederate army that retreated across the border into Georgia would soon outnumber its overconfident foe, the Army of the Cumberland.

For once Rosecrans acted as Washington wanted, rapidly setting his army in motion for an aggressive pursuit of Bragg's troops, whom he now believed to be demoralized and unable to put up a serious fight. In his haste to pursue his foe, he allowed his forces to march south by separate routes with miles between his three corps. One of his corps commanders, Gen. George H. Thomas, warned Rosecrans that it might be wise to consolidate his forces and proceed in a more cautious manner. But Old Rosy couldn't be slowed down by such warnings, especially since a number of Confederate deserters had related to

James Longstreet

their Union captors that Bragg's retreat was a disorganized rout of disheartened men who had all but given up. Little did Rosecrans suspect that these "deserters" had been purposefully sent into the Union lines with their tall tales of Southern defeat. Actually, the Army of Tennessee had remained well organized, withdrawing into Georgia in an orderly fashion. At LaFayette, Georgia, twenty-six miles south of Chattanooga, Bragg built up his army's strength, receiving more than eleven thousand additional troops from Mississippi. Then Bragg welcomed the most formidable reinforcements of all: an entire corps (twelve thousand men) from the Army of Northern Virginia under the command of Robert E. Lee's most trusted subordinate, Lt. Gen. James Longstreet. Longstreet's corps began arriving by railroad, detraining at nearby Ringgold. Suddenly Bragg had troops from one of the toughest armies in

military history: hardened veterans of Gettysburg, some survivors of Pickett's Charge. The best of Lee's legendary force
was at Bragg's disposal; it would be his "ace in the hole" for his
showdown with Rosecrans.

When fully reinforced, the Army of Tennessee could boast
of being sixty-six thousand strong, while the Army of the
Cumberland numbered fifty-eight thousand. General Bragg
became bold and confident (almost as he was so many years
before during the Mexican War) and at last moved to strike his
foe. Twice he tried unsuccessfully to destroy isolated segments
of Rosecrans's army. Then on September 18, he posted his
army on the west bank of Chickamauga Creek, attempting to
wedge his forces between the Army of the Cumberland and the
city of Chattanooga, twelve miles away. The fate of Tennessee
now hung in the balance just across the border in Georgia.
One of the most vicious, costly battles of the entire war was
about to begin near the clearwater stream which the Cherokee
Tribe had ironically named Chickamauga, meaning "River of
Blood."

Fighting began shortly after dawn on September 19 when
Union infantry clashed with now Brig. Gen. Nathan Bedford
Forrest's cavalry at Jay's Mill. This brought on a general
engagement that spread south for nearly four miles. The
armies fought desperately all day, sometimes hand to hand.
Gradually, the Confederates pushed the Federals back to
LaFayette Road. That night, Lt. Gen. James Longstreet arrived
in person with two more brigades from Virginia. Longstreet
and his corps would make the following day of battle a decisive
one.

On September 20 at about 9:30 A.M., Generals Breckinridge
and Cleburne assaulted the Union left, held by Gen. George
H. Thomas's stubborn troops who had built breastworks during the night. Thomas repulsed the heavy assaults as Rosecrans
ordered a division to reinforce him. As fate would have it, this
division was pulled out of the center of the Union line, leaving
a gap, just as Longstreet's battle-hardened troops charged the

The Rock of Chickamauga

same location. The Army of Northern Virginia veterans surged through the gap and totally crushed the Federal right. Half of the Army of the Cumberland suddenly broke and fled from the battlefield in a complete rout! Swept along with the disorderly panic was Rosecrans himself, whose headquarters was overrun by Rebel soldiers. Two of Rosecran's three corps commanders, Generals Alexander McCook and Thomas L. Crittenden, fled as well. They all skedaddled back toward Chattanooga. Longstreet then turned north and struck Thomas's lightly defended flank on Snodgrass Hill. But the stouthearted Thomas patched up his line and repelled the fierce Rebel assaults all afternoon, saving the Army of the Cumberland from total destruction and earning the title "the Rock of Chickamauga."

One of the last Confederate charges of the day included the Fourth Tennessee Cavalry, which participated dismounted in the assault. Among the troopers of the regiment were forty African-Americans who had been serving as camp servants but who now demanded the right to participate in the last combat of the day. Captain J. B. Briggs gave his permission for them to join his command on the front line. Organized and equipped under Daniel McLemore, the personal servant of the colonel of the regiment, the black troops had collected dropped weapons from battlefields during the regiment's campaigns and were prepared to serve the Southern Cause to the fullest. These men, like thousands of other Tennesseans, fought for the defense of their homeland against an invading foe, not for slavery or political ideas. The Fourth participated in one of the final charges against General Thomas's line that bloody day in September, and their little company of Confederate African-American troops suffered four killed and seven wounded.

At sundown, Thomas at last conducted an orderly retreat from the battlefield, heading back to Chattanooga to join the rest of the defeated Army of the Cumberland. General Bragg had just won the most tremendous victory of his career, yet he was overcome by the huge casualty reports. His army, like the Federal army, sustained 28 percent casualties at Chickamauga, the bloodiest two-day battle of the entire war. The Confederates had 2,312 killed, 14,674 wounded, and 1,468 missing, a total of 18,454. The Federals had 1,657 killed, 9,756 wounded, and 4,757 missing, a total of 16,170. Bragg simply would not believe he had won a decisive victory with such huge casualties suffered by his army. To put it in perspective, the French Army under Napoleon was utterly defeated and destroyed at the Battle of Waterloo with 31 percent casualties; not far from what both sides suffered at Chickamauga.

Confederate African-American troops fought bravely at Chickamauga.

Generals Longstreet, Polk, and Forrest argued for Bragg to immediately pursue his routed enemy and recapture Chattanooga while his foe was weak and disorganized. However, Bragg believed his own army was nearly wrecked, and he just shook his head and retired to his tent.

Bragg's march to Chattanooga was slow. The first elements

of his army did not reach the outskirts of the city until two days after the Battle of Chickamauga. However, his main battle for the time period was with his own generals. Disgusted with Bragg's defeatist attitude, ponderous strategy, and terrible disposition, twelve of his senior generals submitted a petition to Pres. Jefferson Davis on October 4, calling for Bragg's removal from command. Included among the signatures were Generals Longstreet, Hill, and Buckner. Generals Polk and Forrest had already had serious run-ins with Bragg and were soon transferred out of the Army of Tennessee. Forrest in particular expressed his honest opinion to Bragg a week after Chickamauga. He told his commander to his face: "I have stood your meanness as long as I intend to. You have played the part of a damned scoundrel, and are a coward, and if you were any part of a man I would slap your jaws. If you ever again try to interfere with me or cross my path it will be at the peril of your life." Bragg, a stickler for discipline, held back from any punitive action against Forrest's insubordination. Nor did he challenge him to a duel, which Forrest may have welcomed. The former slave trader was known to be a hard, dangerous man. No one wanted to be on the wrong side of Nathan Bedford Forrest. Instead of punishment, Forrest was soon promoted to major general and given his own independent cavalry command, separate from the Army of Tennessee. Thus, Bragg escaped his further wrath.

After receiving the generals' petition, President Davis traveled immediately to Bragg's army. He listened to all sides of the arguments and, in the end, chose to retain his old Mexican War buddy, Bragg, in command. Before leaving, Davis gave a bit of military advice, which he obviously expected to be taken since he had come to Bragg's rescue. He recommended detaching Longstreet with fifteen thousand troops for a campaign to retake Knoxville from Burnside's army. Once again the meddling president wiped out a huge fraction of Bragg's army which would be sorely missed in the upcoming struggle. This time it was a quarter of the army's strength that included

Forrest's threats went unchallenged by Bragg.

Longstreet and his tough veterans of the Army of Northern Virginia—the very men who had brought victory for the South at Chickamauga! Their absence at Chattanooga would bring defeat. Davis was proving himself to be invaluable to the Federal Cause.

After Davis left for Richmond, Bragg immediately set to work reorganizing his army. He relieved Hill and Buckner, then reshuffled the units of his three corps. His new corps commanders were Generals Breckinridge (a well-deserved promotion) and Hardee (who was transferred back from Mississippi). Longstreet (whom Bragg still respected) retained most of his original corps and was sent northeast on the ill-fated Knoxville misadventure. Through his reorganization process, Bragg attempted to eradicate dissension in his army's command structure. However, the men in the ranks of the Army of Tennessee had low morale as well as their leaders. They were also dissatisfied with Bragg and his ways. Besides that, rations were short. Though Bragg's strategy was to surround Chattanooga and starve the Yankees out, his own army was even worse off than his foe. Desertions reached a record rate; there were 2,149 troops missing from Bragg's ragtag army in the months of September and October alone.

In his effort to retake Chattanooga, Bragg occupied the high points outside the city, Missionary Ridge and Lookout Mountain. By placing artillery on the heights overlooking the Tennessee River and blocking the roads and rail lines, the Army of Tennessee (or what was left of it) attempted to prevent Federal supplies from entering the city. Bragg's opponent, Rosecrans, had occupied the formidable defenses around Chattanooga which the Confederates themselves had built when they were holding the city. His men further strengthened these positions and waited. Unless the Federal high command did something to break Bragg's siege, the Union army holding Chattanooga would have to surrender or starve.

Aware of the Army of the Cumberland's plight, Federal authorities in Washington ordered reinforcements to its relief.

Late in October, about twenty thousand Union troops of the Army of the Potomac from the front lines in Virginia under Gen. Joseph Hooker muscled their way to the vicinity of Chattanooga. In mid-November, Gen. William T. Sherman arrived with sixteen thousand more troops, fresh from Federal victories in Mississippi. Perhaps just as important as additional troops was the arrival of Maj. Gen. Ulysses S. Grant. The great man of destiny arrived at Federal headquarters in Chattanooga at dusk on October 23, soaking wet and muddy from his rough ride (his horse had slipped in the rain and thrown him).

Grant had just come from a meeting with Secretary of War Edwin Stanton, aboard a train, in which Grant was given orders elevating him to command the newly created Military Division of the Mississippi, a huge area incorporating the various Federal armies operating in the Western Theater. His first duty in his new position was to decide if General Rosecrans would remain in command of the Army of the Cumberland, or if Gen. George H. Thomas, the Rock of Chickamauga, should replace him. With his headquarters overrun at Chickamauga, Rosecrans had had little choice but to flee or face capture, yet it was hard to live down such a humiliating situation, especially since Thomas had remained on the field and fought the rest of the day. Since the battle, Rosecrans had done little other than strengthen his defenses around Chattanooga. President Lincoln considered the general "stunned and confused, like a duck hit on the head." Thus, Grant chose to relieve Rosecrans and replace him with Thomas. The orders were sent by wire ahead of Grant's arrival with instructions for Thomas to "hold Chattanooga at all hazards." Thomas immediately wired back, "We will hold the town till we starve."

Upon Grant's arrival, he and Thomas conferred on strategy. Their immediate concern was supplying Chattanooga. Grant ordered work to begin on opening a supply line, and Thomas's troops cheerfully swung into action, glad to finally be doing something. With the help of a successful amphibious operation on the Tennessee River and some hot skirmishing, especially at Wauhatchie, the route was open by October 28. It was called the "cracker line," since one of the most common food staples for troops was big, hardtack crackers. The cracker line brought vital supplies from the Federally controlled railhead at Bridgeport, Alabama, up the river to Kelly's Ferry aboard steamboats, and then overland into Chattanooga.

Learning of Longstreet's march to Knoxville, Grant began to plan an attack on Bragg's weakened army. It would involve a series of hard blows designed to take the three strategic pieces of high ground in quick succession: Orchard Knob, Lookout Mountain, and Missionary Ridge. Spies and deserters told of the weakened condition of Bragg's army, and Grant decided the time may be right to strike. Actually at this time, Bragg had about forty-four thousand hungry, demoralized troops while Grant had about sixty thousand well-fed, spirited soldiers anxious to bust out of Chattanooga and whip their foes. To test the waters, Grant ordered Thomas and his Army of the Cumberland to make a forced reconnaissance of the Rebel lines. Their objective was Orchard Knob, a hill in front of Missionary Ridge. On November 23, Thomas's troops, anxious to prove their worth after the defeat at Chickamauga, moved out as if on dress parade with drums rolling and banners fluttering and snapping in the wind. The long lines of bluecoats easily drove off the ragged Confederate defenders from their trenches and soon occupied the hill in front of the dark, ominous ridge.

With the positive results of the easy Orchard Knob victory, Grant ordered General Hooker and his three divisions from the Army of the Potomac to assault Lookout Mountain, the anchor of Bragg's left flank, the next day. On the foggy morning of November 24, Hooker's veteran troops bridged Lookout Creek and swept the face of the mountain, working their way up through rocks and tangled growth in the gunsmoke-shrouded woods. The Federals forged ahead, driving a Confederate brigade around the face of the mountain to a plateau. At a farm owned by a family named Cravens, Rebel reinforcements blazed away at the Yanks from behind breastworks beyond the Cravens's house. Misty fog began to thicken and obscure the view of the combatants as well as the observers at the base of the mountain. Flashes of musketry could be seen like fireflies through the murky clouds. Hooker consolidated his gain halfway up the mountain at about 2:00 P.M. as a shortage of ammunition and poor visibility brought an end to the so-called Battle Above the Clouds. During the night the Confederates withdrew from Lookout Mountain and reported to Bragg on Missionary Ridge. The next morning, the rising sun burned away the fog to reveal a huge U.S. flag flying at the mountain's summit.

Grant's plan for the following day called for Sherman and his men, on the Federal left, to assault the north end of Missionary Ridge, while Hooker and his troops, on the Federal right, stormed Rossville Gap on the south end of the ridge as Thomas and his Army of the Cumberland simply held their position in the center of the Federal line. Sherman's assault began as scheduled on the morning of the twenty-fifth. But his troops ran into a virtual wall; namely the "Stonewall Jackson of the West," Gen. Pat Cleburne. Cleburne and his division were determined to hold the Yanks back as charge after charge failed to dislodge the hardened Southerners from their defense of Tunnel Hill (a railroad tunnel cut through the hill on the north end of Missionary Ridge). The Confederates even launched a furious counterattack with Cleburne himself in the lead flourishing his sword like an Irish warrior of old.

Meanwhile, Hooker and his men, on the other side of the ridge, ran into delays in their attempt to cross Chattanooga Creek. The bridge had been destroyed, and Rossville Road was obstructed by the Confederates. The Federal plan to take Missionary Ridge was falling apart. To create a diversion and relieve pressure on his faltering attacks, Grant ordered Thomas to send his men forward to take only the first line of Confederate trenches at the base of Missionary Ridge. Four divisions, twenty thousand men, of the Army of the

The Battle Above the Clouds

Cumberland, still itching to prove themselves to be brave soldiers, charged fearlessly forward.

General Bragg had ordered his troops manning the first line of defense at the base of the ridge to fire only once, then fall back up the slope. This they did, and Thomas's exultant troops pursued the retreating Southerners. Confederate troops in the successive defenses had trouble firing at their foes for fear of hitting their comrades who were skedaddling right in front of the pursuing Federals. Thomas's victorious troops had paused only briefly before charging right up the face of the sloping ridge without orders! Observing the incredible sight through his field glasses at the Federal command post set up atop Orchard Knob, Grant angrily turned to Thomas and barked, "Thomas, who ordered those men up the ridge?" The "Rock" replied that he didn't know. The massive, impromptu, frontal assault climbed up the rough face of Missionary Ridge as a ragged wall of frantic gray-clad troops scurried in front of an uneven, surging sea of blue-clad soldiers shouting a vengeful battle cry over and over: "Chickamauga, Chickamauga, CHICKAMAUGA!" Defensive fire from the nervous Rebels was sporadic as their own comrades unwittingly shielded their foes as they ran to the summit of the ridge. Yet many a brave young Yank took a bullet on that rugged slope as the blue masses moved onward toward the crest.

Three color-bearers of the Twenty-Fourth Wisconsin, part of Gen. Phil Sheridan's division, were shot down in quick succession. Lieutenant Arthur MacArthur Jr. picked up the flag and shouted, "On Wisconsin!" The young officer plunged forward, followed by the regiment's troops all the way to the crest of the ridge, where the Confederate defenders broke and ran. For his gallantry that day, MacArthur won the Congressional Medal of Honor, an inspiration in later years to his son, Gen. Douglas MacArthur. All along the summit of Missionary Ridge, the ragged, hungry, demoralized troops of Braxton Bragg fell back in the face of the furious, vengeful assault of the Army of the Cumberland's troops shouting their battle cry of retribution.

Their amazing, spontaneous charge is considered to be one of the most miraculous events of the entire war.

Just as Rosecrans's headquarters was overrun at Chickamauga, now Bragg's headquarters was overrun at Missionary Ridge. Private Sam Watkins was among those Confederates who scurried up the ridge in front of the Federal charge. He recalled the day vividly: "There was no firing from the Rebel lines in our immediate front. They [the Federals] kept climbing and pulling and scratching until I was in touching distance of the old Rebel breastworks, right on the very apex of Missionary Ridge. I made one jump, and I heard Captain Turner, who had the very four Napoleon guns we had captured at Perryville, halloo out, 'Number four, solid!' and then a roar [the artillery had been waiting for Watkins and his fellow soldiers to get out of the way]. The next order was 'Limber to the rear.' The Yankees were cutting and slashing, and the cannoneers were running in every direction. I saw Day's brigade throw down their guns and break like quarter horses. Bragg was trying to rally them. I heard him say 'Here is your commander,' and the soldiers hallooed back 'here is your mule' [a common military jeer during the war]."

Like Rosecrans at Chickamauga, Bragg at Missionary Ridge had little choice but to flee or face capture. The center of his line was broken and routed, fleeing down the eastern slope of the ridge. Meanwhile, back at the north end of the ridge, Cleburne's men were actually cheering their success over Sherman's troops when their corps commander, General Hardee, rode up and announced the collapse of the Confederate center, warning Cleburne he was in danger of being flanked. The Irishman was the only Confederate general in the battle whose force had not been routed, so he and his men were assigned to protect the retreat of the Army of Tennessee, which marched to Chickamauga Station during the night. By rail and on foot, Bragg's demoralized troops escaped deeper into Georgia, eluding the pursuing Federals. Grant called an end to the pursuit on November 28, the day after

*Bragg yelled, "Here is your commander." His men replied,
"Here's your mule!"*

Cleburne stung the Yanks bad at a mountain pass outside
Ringgold, Georgia.

The Battles of Orchard Knob, Lookout Mountain, and

Missionary Ridge, known collectively as the Battle of Chattanooga, put Tennessee in the firm grip of the Federal government. Chattanooga also resulted in major changes in the command structure of both the Union and Confederate Armies. Bragg requested to be relieved of command and went to Richmond to become President Davis's military advisor. Davis turned command of the Army of Tennessee over to Gen. Joseph E. Johnston, who would oppose General Sherman's advance into Georgia the following year. As a direct result of the great Chattanooga victory, Grant would be promoted by President Lincoln in March of the following year to General in Chief, commanding all Union armies in the field. He would go East to personally oppose General Lee and his Army of Northern Virginia. Casualties in the dramatic and strategically important struggle for Chattanooga were light compared to the bloodbath of Chickamauga. The Union forces lost 687 killed, 4,346 wounded, and 349 captured or missing. The Confederates lost 361 killed, 2,160 wounded, and 4,146 captured or missing.

Just before the Battle of Chattanooga, a twenty-one-year-old Confederate private, Sam Davis, was captured near the town of Pulaski and taken to the headquarters of occupying Federal troops. Davis was a member of a unit known as Coleman's Scouts, and he carried a pass signed "E. Coleman" which allowed him through Confederate military lines to see General Bragg. Papers for Bragg were found under his saddle and in his boot that gave valuable information on Federal positions, troop numbers, and movements. One paper was a monthly report taken directly from the desk of Davis's interrogator, Brig. Gen. Grenville Dodge. Dodge offered young Davis his freedom if he would name his informants and give information on the location of his commander, Capt. Henry Shaw (a wanted man by the Federals). Handsome young Davis remained silent, and Dodge turned him over to a court-martial board to be tried as a military spy. The board, which convened on November 24 (as the Battle of Lookout Mountain raged), found Davis guilty and sentenced him to be hanged on November 27. General Dodge, who admired the brave youthful Rebel's courage, offered repeatedly to commute his death sentence if he would cooperate. However, Sam Davis held his tongue, even when he stood on the scaffold and was made one final offer of life in exchange for betrayal. His reply (perhaps in a bit more formal form than Sam's actual wording) is engraved on the base of his statue on the courthouse square in present-day Pulaski: "If I had a thousand lives, I would lose them all here before I would betray my friend or the confidence of my informer." The youthful soldier who came to be known as "the Boy Martyr of the Confederacy," was executed that day in Pulaski. Many years later, one of the numerous contributors to a monument honoring Sam Davis was none other than an aging, former Union general, Grenville Dodge.

Meanwhile, far to the northeast, General Longstreet and his force had reached their objective, Knoxville. General Burnside and his men found themselves besieged but secure behind strong fortifications. Also, the pro-Union populace of Knoxville kept the boys in blue well fed. This was the first serious challenge to Burnside and his Army of the Ohio since they had taken possession of Knoxville. Earlier, however, they had been harassed by a Confederate cavalry force that crossed the border from southwest Virginia under the command of Brig. Gen. John S. Williams. This contact resulted in some minor skirmishing until the Yanks drove off Williams and his men in a sharp fight at Blue Springs on October 10. Burnside's bloodless capture of Knoxville and the subsequent, more violent, effort to hold it for the Union came to be known as the East Tennessee Campaign.

General Longstreet received a message from Bragg on the night of November 23 (during the Battle of Chattanooga) that stated if it was possible to defeat Burnside it must be done immediately, without a long siege. Longstreet scheduled an attack on the Federal works for sunrise on the twenty-fifth, but, learning of the approach of two more infantry brigades from

He would rather die than betray a friend.

Bragg as reinforcements, he postponed the assault. The arrival of the additional troops resulted in a surprise night assault on November 28 by four brigades against a sector of the Federal works protected by an earthenwork defense known as Fort

Sanders. As freezing sleet pelted their faces, the Confederates advanced and captured or drove in the Federal pickets, taking possession of abandoned trenches within 150 yards of the grim dirt fort. The gunfire alerted the 440 Union troops posted at Fort Sanders, as cannoneers rushed to their posts, manning the twelve artillery pieces emplaced behind the earthen ramparts. Throughout the night, the big guns fired charges of canister toward their unseen attackers as more Union troops were shifted to the Fort Sanders sector to bolster its strength.

At dawn on November 29, Col. E. Porter Alexander, the young Confederate artillery officer who had directed the bombardment of Cemetery Ridge at Gettysburg only a little more than four months earlier, opened fire on Fort Sanders with his gun batteries. Alexander had little time to bombard the fort as the troops of Maj. Gen. Lafayette McLaws, one of Longstreet's division commanders, surged forward in a grand assault. As they neared the fort, McLaws's men encountered a nasty surprise; wire entanglements had been put in place a few inches above the ground, secured to stumps and stakes. It was perhaps the first time in military history that troops in combat encountered such defensive obstacles as they attempted to move forward. Telegraph wire was utilized since barbed wire had not yet been invented. The new innovation disordered the ranks and slowed the assault, allowing riflemen and cannoneers from inside the fort to claim more targets. The deadly hail of gunfire mowed down scores of brave young Rebels who scrambled desperately through the wire entanglements toward the earthen walls where countless fiery muzzle flashes could be seen through the thick, swirling clouds of gunsmoke. Some reached the fort's dry moat, only to be slaughtered by rifle fire and crude grenades made from lighting fuses on cannonballs and tossing them over the wall. As McLaws's men withdrew, another desperate charge was launched, this time by troops from Gen. Micah Jenkins's division, but the gory, futile results were the same. The assault had cost the Confederates more than 800 casualties: 129 killed, 458 wounded, and 226 missing. Total Union losses were only about a score.

Plans for a better organized attack were made, but before it was launched, dispatches were received at Longstreet's headquarters confirming the rumors that had already been circulating about Bragg's disastrous defeat and his retreat beyond Ringgold, Georgia. Orders were received for Longstreet to end his siege. However, reports were also received of the approach of Gen. William T. Sherman and a strong column of Union troops, who had been sent by Grant (after his victory at Chattanooga) to save Burnside and his besieged troops. Therefore, Longstreet decided it was best to hold his ground for awhile to draw the Union force farther away from Bragg toward Knoxville. The Army of Northern Virginia veterans held firm until December 3 when Sherman's vanguard was within a day's march. During the night, Longstreet's supply wagons started rolling northeast. The troops followed the next day, ending the sixteen-day siege and marching to Russellville where they went into winter quarters. Early the following spring, they would leave Tennessee forever. Thus, 1863 came to an end with the state of Tennessee in the firm grip of the Federal government.

Small detachments of Confederate cavalry and guerrillas that dared to remain behind in Tennessee found themselves to be the hunted prey of strong patrols of Federal troops seeking out their camps and bases of operation. On December 10, a patrol of the Fifteenth Pennsylvania Cavalry surprised a camp of Cherokee troops of the Thomas Legion along a ridge near Gatlinburg. Four hours of skirmishing ensued in which the cavalry troopers drove Colonel Thomas and his retreating Cherokees deep into the rugged Smoky Mountains. The Confederate camp was burned, and one Indian, fifteen horses, and twenty rifles were seized.

CHAPTER 4

Hard March to Destiny: 1864-65

The year 1864 began with a tense, uneasy silence in Tennessee. To the south, at Dalton, Georgia, the Army of Tennessee (with about fifty thousand troops) under Gen. Joseph E. Johnston prepared for the coming storm of combat. In Chattanooga, the Military Division of the Mississippi (with about a hundred thousand troops) under Maj. Gen. William T. Sherman prepared to invade Georgia. In desperate need of support, Johnston relied heavily on the talents of the region's Confederate cavalry units to disrupt the flow of Union supplies, cut lines of communication, destroy railroads used by the Federals, and generally make life miserable for the Yankees. As a result, the new year's silence in Tennessee was soon broken by the ominous rumble of thousands of hoofbeats pounding the earth and the sharp crack of gunfire, rattling sabers, and Rebel yells. A series of lightning cavalry raids set the state ablaze with violence as the leather-tough troopers of Generals Forrest, Wheeler, and Morgan rode hard across the land.

True to character, Nathan Bedford Forrest was the first to strike. During his raid, he fought one of the most infamous and controversial actions of the entire war—the Battle of Fort Pillow. The fort had been occupied by Federal troops since it was abandoned by the Confederates in 1862. In the spring of

1864 there were more than 550 Union soldiers at the post: an undersized regiment of Union Tennessee troops and four companies of African-American artillerymen. On the night of April 11, fifteen hundred Confederate cavalry troopers surrounded the small fort as shots were exchanged in the darkness. The next morning Forrest sent a messenger under a flag of truce into the post with a demand of its surrender. The fort refused to capitulate without a fight, and Forrest ordered his men to charge. The Union troops were soon overwhelmed as the dismounted cavalry raiders swarmed over the parapets in a flurry of gunfire. What happened next became the subject of heated debate for more than a hundred years.

Union survivors of the battle recalled witnessing scores of their comrades, mainly African-Americans, gunned down after surrendering. Confederates claimed that in the confusion of the action, some Union soldiers were still firing as others were surrendering, and it was necessary to continue to shoot into the Union ranks in self-defense. After studying the evidence gathered for more than a century, most historians today believe atrocities were indeed committed at Fort Pillow although the massacre was limited, not total. It is also now generally accepted that Forrest himself did not direct or condone the slaughter. As any war veteran can attest, the line between man and beast sometimes wears very thin in the midst of deadly combat.

The casualty figures from Fort Pillow always did reveal the true story: the Confederates had 14 killed, the Federals suffered about 230 killed (mainly African-Americans). The sight of black Union troops enraged Confederates like nothing else. The idea of former loyal servants joining a bloody slave uprising against the Southland was abhorrent to them. Regardless of whether or not Forrest himself had a role in the killing of prisoners, the horror of Fort Pillow magnified his reputation as a deadly, merciless warrior to be feared by his foes.

The next day, April 13, the Union gunboat *Silver Cloud* arrived and began to bombard the fort. The Confederates

The bloody legacy of Fort Pillow

agreed to allow wounded Federal soldiers (about a hundred of them) to be evacuated. Forrest's men left soon afterward to threaten Columbus and Paducah, Kentucky, before heading back south. Neither side occupied the bloody grounds of Fort Pillow again.

In early may, Sherman's invasion of Georgia was underway. As he pushed his way deeper into the beleaguered state,

Sherman became increasingly concerned about his lengthening supply line. Specifically, the stern Yankee general worried about Forrest's devastating raids into Tennessee cutting off the supplies needed by his massive force which actually consisted of three armies: Army of the Cumberland, Army of the Ohio, and Army of the Tennessee (Union). Sherman sent a force of more than eight thousand troops into Mississippi to seek out and destroy Forrest's cavalry before he could launch another Tennessee raid. On June 10, Forrest's thirty-five hundred troopers clashed with the Union force at Brice's Crossroads near Tishomingo Creek and totally routed the Yanks in a brilliant victory. Frustrated, Sherman sent a larger force of fourteen thousand troops on another seek-and-destroy mission against Forrest. "Forrest is the very devil," Sherman wrote, and he resolved to "follow Forrest to the death, if it cost 10,000 lives and breaks the treasury. There will never be peace in Tennessee till Forrest is dead." On July 14, the overwhelming numbers of Union troops defeated, but could not destroy, Forrest's command at Tupelo, Mississippi, wounding Forrest himself. Thus, the feared Confederate raider was temporarily put in check, but he would not stay down for long.

Meanwhile, back in Georgia, the Army of Tennessee under Gen. Joe Johnston was slowly driven back toward Atlanta as Sherman's massive juggernaut rumbled forward. Johnston used defensive, delaying tactics as best he could in the face of overwhelming odds; he even scored a morale-boosting victory at Kennesaw Mountain on June 27. However, President Davis and many other Southerners wanted Johnston to be more aggressive and even go on the offensive against the invading Union armies. Fearful that Johnston would abandon Atlanta without a fight, Davis took the advice of his military advisor, Gen. Braxton Bragg, and replaced him on July 18. The new commander of the Army of Tennessee, Gen. John Bell Hood, had the reputation of being one of the toughest fighting officers in the Confederacy—but not a skilled strategist or tactician. Hood had been a division commander in Longstreet's corps of the Army of Northern Virginia. He had been schooled in offensive tactics while campaigning with Gen. Robert E. Lee and had come west with Longstreet to Tennessee for the Battle of Chickamauga. His shattered and useless left arm was still in a sling from a crippling wound at Gettysburg when he was struck by a bullet that cost him his right leg at Chickamauga. He had retained his assignment to the Army of Tennessee while recovering from the leg amputation in Richmond. Upon his return to the field, he was a corps commander under Johnston during the beginning of the Atlanta Campaign. His horrible, crippling wounds (he had to be strapped to his saddle to keep from falling off) had failed to abate his aggressive, fighting nature.

President Davis had asked General Lee (who knew Hood well) for his opinion on the idea of giving Hood overall command in Georgia, and Lee had advised against it, stating that Hood was "all lion, none of the fox." Yet the meddling president once again did as he pleased against sound advice, much to the delight of General Sherman who stated he was "pleased at this change." Private Sam Watkins of the First Tennessee recalled the reaction of his fellow soldiers to the change in command: "The most terrible and disastrous blow that the South ever received was when Hon. Jefferson Davis placed General Hood in command of the Army of Tennessee. I saw, I will say, thousands of men cry like babies—regular, old-fashioned boohoo, boohoo, boohoo."

After taking over, Hood sent his army's cavalry, under "Fighting Joe" Wheeler, on a spectacular raid against Federal communications and supply lines in Tennessee. On August 10, Wheeler and his forty-five hundred troopers rode north. They crossed the Little Tennessee and passed north of Knoxville, destroying bridges and tracks. Wheeler's raiders then tore up the railroad west of McMinnville, passing then to the Nashville and Decatur Road near Franklin, and finally crossing the Tennessee River to rejoin Hood's army. Wheeler returned with barely two thousand men and found that his cavalry's absence

Hood gave his all for the South, but he was "all lion, none of the fox."

had led to the loss of Atlanta. At the Battle of Jonesboro on August 31 and September 1, Sherman was able to outflank Hood (because he had no cavalry) and take his rail supply line twenty miles south of Atlanta. Hood then had no choice but to abandon the city on the night of September 1 after blowing up or burning everything of military value. Sherman's victorious troops marched into the city the next day.

Early September of 1864 was a tragic time period for the Confederacy. Not only did the South lose Atlanta, it also lost one of its best cavalry commanders. On the night of September 4, a Union cavalry detachment surrounded the town of Greeneville, Tennessee, in an attempt to capture Gen. John H. Morgan. Morgan had made a dramatic escape from the Ohio State Penitentiary the previous November where he had been held as a prisoner of war after his astonishing raid through southern Indiana and Ohio. He had no intention of becoming a prisoner again. In his attempt to escape the trap at Greeneville, the dashing Morgan was shot dead near the courthouse square at the Williams family home. A stone marker placed near the site stands today on the courthouse lawn in Greeneville.

After losing Atlanta, Hood had to decide what course of action to take next. From the Confederate viewpoint, the major military disaster in Georgia had already taken place with the loss of Atlanta, a city which most Southerners considered to be second in importance only to Richmond itself. Hood chose to flank Sherman's forces and move north, getting in the rear of the Federal juggernaut where he would attempt to cut Sherman's supply lines. In support came none other than the amazing Nathan Bedford Forrest who once again launched a raid into Tennessee in late September. His hard-riding troopers went as far north as Spring Hill. They wrecked the Nashville and Decatur Railroad, immobilized about fifteen thousand Federal troops, and captured large quantities of horses and stores. Forrest eluded the large contingents of Federal troops attempting to trap his force and withdrew to northern Mississippi, arriving in early October.

At the end of October, Major General Forrest carried out one of the most incredible raids of the war. His target was a huge Federal supply depot located on the Tennessee River at Johnsonville, south of old Fort Henry. For several days he lobbed artillery projectiles at Union supply boats along the river, then on the night of November 3, he positioned his artillery on high ground directly across the river from the Federal fort, river port, and supply depot. The next day, his resulting bombardment caused nearly unbelievable destruction. Forrest's Johnsonville Raid resulted in the burning and/or sinking of four gunboats, fourteen steamboats, and seventeen loaded barges. The inferno resulting from his artillery barrage engulfed at least seventy-five thousand tons of Federal supplies. Forrest's men also captured 150 prisoners. Confederate losses at Johnsonville totaled two killed and nine wounded.

On October 5, Forrest led his command toward northern Alabama where he had orders to report to General Hood. Hood's army was preparing for an invasion of Tennessee in an effort to draw Sherman's forces north out of Georgia. Hood had gotten the approval of President Davis for his audacious plan to leave Georgia and march into Tennessee via northern Alabama. Even if Sherman failed to pursue, Hood reasoned he could retake the state with his forty thousand men and maybe even enter Kentucky and threaten Ohio, or perhaps march on into Virginia in support of General Lee who was struggling with the tenacious Grant. Hood had left all his cavalry, under General Wheeler, in Georgia to harass Sherman, and ordered Forrest's command to join him as a replacement.

Meanwhile, Sherman had already sent troops into Tennessee to contend with Hood since his invasion plan was obvious due to his massing of troops in northern Alabama. Sherman eventually would order approximately seventy thousand Federal troops into Tennessee to oppose Hood's army. He had already sent Gen. George H. Thomas to Nashville as overall U.S. commander in the state and had sent additional troops with young Maj. Gen. John M. Schofield who set up his headquarters at Pulaski. As for Sherman's Georgia Campaign, he had received approval from Grant and Lincoln to proceed with a grand "March to the Sea" with Savannah as his final objective. Thus, in November of 1864, America witnessed the strange sight of the two contending generals, Sherman and Hood, simply turning their backs on each other and marching off in opposite directions. The "Volunteer State" would once again endure the horrors of full-scale war as the Army of Tennessee marched back across her southern border.

The three corps of Hood's army entered Tennessee in separate columns: one under Maj. Gen. Benjamin F. Cheatham, another under Lt. Gen. Alexander Stewart, and a third under Lt. Gen. Stephen D. Lee. Soon after crossing the border into Tennessee, the troops were given a rousing welcoming speech by Governor-in-exile Isham Harris, who was riding as an aide to Hood. Meanwhile, General Schofield, with about twenty-eight thousand men of the Fourth and Twenty-Third Corps of the Army of the Tennessee (Union), withdrew before the Confederate advance, with orders to join General Thomas at Nashville. Schofield's force reached Columbia and the bridge over Duck River just in time to prevent its seizure by Forrest's cavalry. Hood was attempting to overtake Schofield and defeat his force before it had a chance to reinforce Thomas at Nashville. Confederates crossed Duck River about five miles east of Columbia and made a rapid, forced march to Spring Hill over back roads. For awhile it looked as if Hood's attempt to intercept Schofield at Spring Hill would succeed.

Some deadly skirmishing took place at Spring Hill on the afternoon of November 29 as Forrest's cavalry, and later Cleburne's division, assaulted Union troops near the village. As dusk arrived, Hood's entire army drew closer and camped for the night. However, under cover of darkness, Schofield's entire Federal force pulled off one of the most amazing escape maneuvers of the war, quietly shuffling by Hood's advance units and marching to Franklin, only about twenty miles south of Nashville. There the Yanks stopped to briefly rest, chow down on rations, and repair two bridges they needed to cross the Harpeth River north of town. They rapidly strengthened a defensive line of earthworks in a semicircle around the land approach to the town (defenses constructed a year and a half earlier) and nervously awaited the arrival of their foes. The remainder of Franklin was bordered by a bend in the Harpeth River. The Yanks' only escape route was the two bridges hastily being repaired.

Hood, enraged at his own troops for allowing the Federals to slip away at Spring Hill, drove his army in hot pursuit of Schofield on the morning of the thirtieth, arriving before the grimacing dirt walls and grave-like trenches at Franklin shortly after noon. There was a break in the freezing weather, and the mild afternoon typified "Indian Summer." It would have been a nice day for anything but cruel, bloody warfare. Hood studied the Federal lines through his field glasses, standing on his crutches under a tree. He knew this was his last chance to stop Schofield before he made it to the defenses of Nashville. The grim general planned a massive frontal assault—the old-fashioned, headlong charge that he had always preferred throughout his military career. He was not a tactician; he was a slugger who believed in the power of a furious, ancient, Celtic-style attack with men face to face with their foes. Generals Forrest and Cheatham both voiced their objections to Hood's slaughterous plan. But the hard-hearted warrior had his mind made up. Without waiting for his third corps under Stephen Lee or for most of his artillery, which was still hours away, Hood ordered Cheatham and Stewart to attack. The assault would have to cross two miles of open ground. No fences or groves of trees obstructed the Federals' field of fire. One of the division commanders who would play a major role in the upcoming assault, Maj. Gen. Patrick Cleburne, seemed especially despondent to one of his brigade commanders and fellow Arkansan, Brig. Gen. Daniel C. Govan. After receiving his orders from Cleburne, Govan remarked to his commander that there would not be many left to return to Arkansas. He vividly remembered Cleburne's shocking reply: "Well, Govan, if we are to die, let us die like men."

Twenty-two thousand Confederate infantrymen marched into the two-mile clearing before Franklin's defenses in perfect battle lines with military bands playing patriotic Southern tunes and a hundred battle flags floating above the sea of soldiers. It was 4:00 P.M. when the grand assault began. The beautiful parade-like scene was soon transformed into a nightmare of carnage as the Federal artillery opened fire. Yet cannons alone could not stop the relentless advance of the Army of Tennessee. As the long lines of Confederate infantry drew closer to their objective, two Union brigades, in front of the center of the defenses, were overwhelmed by the Southern tidal wave and raced back toward the trenches. The fearless boys in gray were right on their heels, causing the Yanks in the center of the main Union line to hold their fire for fear of shooting their own men. Then when the skedaddling troops in blue were out of the way, the Union line exploded with rifle and cannon fire, leveling several ranks of Rebels. But the momentum of the fierce charge could not be stopped, and the Confederates broke through the center of the defenses near the house of the Carter family, who huddled in their cellar as bullets rained against the brick walls of their home. In the thick of battle, young Capt. Theodoric Carter, an aide in Cheatham's corps, fell mortally wounded within sight of his family's house.

Union colonel Emerson Opdycke stood aghast at the sight of the Confederate breakthrough. He was in command of a brigade held in reserve behind the now broken center. He immediately hurled his unit into the fray in a desperate attempt to plug the gap in the Federal line. The Eighty-Eighth Illinois Infantry led the charge of Opdycke's brigade and ran head-on into the First and Fourth Missouri Infantry, part of Brig. Gen. Francis M. Cockrell's Confederate Missouri Brigade. Opdycke's men, in furious combat centered around the Carter house and cotton gin, drove back the Confederates

Hand-to-hand fighting at Franklin

with the aid of two other units. It was in the horrific fighting on the Carter land that General Cleburne had a horse shot out from under him. The general immediately received another horse from one of his messengers. He had one leg in the stirrup, preparing to mount, when that horse also went down, struck by an artillery projectile. At that point, General Govan remembered seeing the tough Irish-American commander draw his sword and dash forward on foot: "He then disappeared in the smoke of battle and that was the last time I ever saw him alive."

Charge after charge slammed like human sledgehammers against the Federal defenses. Horrendous hand-to-hand combat ensued—some of the worst close combat of the entire war. Fighting raged around the earthworks with many troops pinned down, hugging dirt walls with their foes only a few feet away on the opposite side of the same walls. Men raised their weapons up with one hand to the top of the mounds of dirt and fired, opposing rifles sometimes striking each other. The

Cleburne disappeared into the smoke of battle.

horrible slaughter continued as dusk faded into night. Finally the gunfire slackened about 9:00 P.M. as the Confederates withdrew. By 11:00 P.M., Schofield had his forces crossing the Harpeth River on the newly repaired bridges which were set afire as soon as his troops completed their escape. He and his army would reach Nashville by noon the next day. Sam Watkins described the devastation left behind at Franklin: "We passed the night where we were. But when the morrow's sun began to light up the eastern sky with its rosy hues, and we looked over the battlefield, O, my God! what did we see! It was a grand holocaust of death. Death had held high carnival there that night. The dead were piled the one on the other all over the ground. I never was so horrified and appalled in my life. Horses, like men, had died game on the gory breastworks. General Adams' [Brig. Gen. John Adams's] horse had his fore feet on one side of the works and his hind feet on the other, dead. The general seems to have been caught so that he was held to the horse's back, sitting almost as if living, riddled, and mangled, and torn with balls. General Cleburne's body was pierced with forty-nine bullets, through and through. General Strahl's [Brig. Gen. Otho Strahl's] horse lay by the roadside and the general by his side, both dead, and all his staff. General Gist [Brig. Gen. States Rights Gist], a noble and brave cavalier from South Carolina, was lying with his sword reaching across the breastworks still grasped in his hand. He was lying there dead. All dead!"

The command structure of the Army of Tennessee was wrecked at Franklin. Among the Confederate casualties were twelve generals: six killed, five wounded, and one captured. A total of fifty-four regimental commanders were casualties. Hood's outdated method of fighting had brought a major disaster to the Southern Cause. He lost an irreplaceable 6,654 casualties: 1,750 killed, 3,800 wounded, and 1,104 captured or missing. Federal losses at Franklin were 189 killed, 1,033 wounded, and 1,104 captured or missing. Schofield's arrival at Nashville brought Thomas's strength up to about seventy thousand men (counting other reinforcements he had received). Although Hood still planned to fight the Federals at Nashville, his chances of a successful campaign were literally shot to pieces at the bloody Battle of Franklin.

After burying the dead, Hood marched the badly battered and demoralized Army of Tennessee to Nashville. There he established an entrenched line on the hills south of the city and the Siege of Nashville began. Actually it was not a "siege" in the true sense of the word; Hood had fewer men than Thomas and did not have the city surrounded or cut off from supplies and reinforcements. The stubborn Confederate commander simply fortified his position and waited for the Federals to assault, hoping to decimate them in the same way they had shattered his army at Franklin. But Thomas was too clever for that. "The Rock" carefully planned his strategy. However, Washington became impatient with his delays and began sending telegrams (mostly from Grant) urging him to attack Hood's position at once. Winter storms on December 8-13 delayed Thomas's assault further, and Grant's patience wore thin. There was a fear that Hood would sideslip Thomas and get into Kentucky or even Ohio. Finally, Maj. Gen. John A. Logan (one of Grant's favorites) was sent on his way from Washington to Nashville to replace the methodical Thomas. However, the Rock stoically waited out the freezing rain, sleet, and snow, and on December 14 there was finally a break in the weather. On December 15, before General Logan arrived to replace him (plus even Grant himself was on his way to personally oversee the operations), Thomas launched his grand assault.

The Rock's battle plan called for one infantry division, including two brigades of African-American troops (who had recently marched into Nashville as welcome reinforcements), to pin down Hood's right with a limited attack, while three entire corps of infantry and all the Federal cavalry smashed Hood's left flank with an all-out assault. On December 15, the morning fog lifted to reveal fifty thousand Federal troops marching from their Nashville defenses toward the Confederate earthworks four miles south of town. With bugles blaring, drums rolling, and flags fluttering in the cold winter air, the blue-coated army steadily advanced toward its foe.

The Army of Tennessee now had only about twenty-five thousand ragged, demoralized troops to defend their dirt walls and trenches in the hills south of Tennessee's capital. Hood had depleted his army even more after Franklin by sending Forrest and most of his cavalry thirty miles away to keep a small Union force in check at Murfreesboro. Forrest would be sorely missed in the upcoming battle. The all-too-familiar sounds of deadly combat once again rang in the ears of Hood's troops as the roar of artillery and crashing volleys of musketry reverberated in the hills south of Nashville. All day long the battered Rebels hung on desperately to their positions against the feinting attacks on their right and the knockout assaults on their left. Hood had no reserves and no interior lines to shift troops to hot spots without leaving dangerous gaps. His forces were spread too thin on a broad front. At dusk the Confederate left finally began to give way, and Hood pulled his shot-up army back two miles to a shorter line anchored by two pieces of high ground: Overton Hill and what would become known as Shy's Hill. Troops on both sides spent a freezing, agonizing night wondering what fate held for them on the morrow.

In the early morning hours of December 16, the Federals reformed their lines of battle and cautiously but confidently advanced. Thick mud slowed their progress, but they finally made contact with Hood's new defensive line and ponderously renewed the same tactics that had given them a victory the day before. The tired, hungry, ragged troops of the South tenaciously defended their new position, and at 3:00 P.M. they even drove back a major assault on Overton Hill with heavy losses to the Yanks. However, soon after the Overton Hill repulse, the Federal cavalry, under their tough commander Bvt. Maj. Gen. James H. Wilson, succeeded in getting in the rear of Hood's left flank. The cavalry troopers made good use of their rapid-firing carbines in a dismounted assault at the same time two infantry corps hit the left flank head-on. By 4:00 P.M. the Confederate left was crushed, and Hood's entire line became untenable. A cold rain was falling as the sun sank low on the horizon, and entire brigades of Confederate troops began to crumble away from the line like a long row of falling dominoes. Thousands of Rebels threw down their weapons and raised their hands in surrender; thousands of others fled southward to the village of Brentwood as Hood's Army of Tennessee abandoned the battlefield in confusion and panic. However, a complete rout was prevented by Gen. Stephen Lee's Corps from the Confederate right. Lee himself grabbed a battle flag and rallied his troops who put up a stubborn resistance to pursuing Federals in a fighting retreat along the pike to Brentwood.

Historians consider the Battle of Nashville to be one of the most decisive actions of the entire Civil War because the utter defeat of the Army of Tennessee signaled the beginning of the fall of the Confederacy. Southern casualties in the two-day battle were estimated to be approximately 1,500 killed and wounded and 4,462 captured or missing. Federal losses were 387 killed, 2,558 wounded, and 112 captured or missing. Union records report Thomas's men also captured seventy-two artillery pieces and three thousand small arms. Hood's invasion of Tennessee had come to a dramatic end with a smashing Union victory at the state capital. The significance of the victory at Nashville is summed up in the words of Pvt. D. T. Gordon of the Thirty-First Indiana Volunteers in a letter to his brother: "We have been in two heavy battles but all of the boys that went with me went through safe. We had to charge the breastworks. It was a big undertaking but I went over the breastwork the first thing I done. The bullets whistled around my head as thick as ever you seen, while the dirt filled my eyes full of dirt so that I could not see where I was going. . . . We took a great many prisoners and guns. We tore old Hood's

For thousands of Southerners, the war was over.

army all to pieces, I don't think they will ever do anything more."

The Confederates' march from Brentwood to Columbia, Tennessee, entailed a nearly continuous rear guard action with pursuing Federal troops. At Columbia, General Forrest, returning from Murfreesboro, linked up with the retreating column and took over as rear guard commander on December 19. Besides his cavalry, Forrest also was given an infantry force to aid in the task of holding off the Federals. The rear guard infantry was made up of the remnants of four brigades under the immediate command of Maj. Gen. Edward C. Walthall. At least a fourth of Walthall's ragged foot soldiers had no shoes. Forrest transported them by wagons; when called upon to fight, they would unload from the wagons and form into a line of battle. Every creek and stream became a skirmish site as the rear guard would make a stand and then fall back, allowing what was left of the Army of Tennessee to escape farther south. Wilson's cavalry pressed the Southerners hard, and finally, two days after Christmas, their broken army reached the Tennessee River where it meanders below the Alabama border. There, Forrest's troopers drove Wilson's men back two miles while Hood's surviving veterans made it safely across the river. Forrest's troopers then rapidly withdrew under the covering fire of Walthall's infantry. General Thomas at last called off the chase at the Tennessee River. The hungry, ragged, whipped Rebels trudged on to their base at Tupelo, Mississippi. The Civil War in Tennessee was finally over.

By the beginning of 1865, the last survivors of Hood's disastrous Tennessee Campaign had straggled into Tupelo, and a head count was taken. Barely half of the forty thousand who had marched north seven weeks earlier had returned. Hood himself survived, but his spirit was broken. He sent a letter of resignation off to Richmond on January 13. Ten days later, President Davis complied with his request.

The surviving fragments of the Army of Tennessee, after refitting and reorganizing at Tupelo, went off to North

Carolina to reinforce their beloved old commander, Gen. Joe Johnston, in his desperate attempt to stop General Sherman's army after his capture of Savannah, Georgia, and Columbia, South Carolina. But it was now a "Lost Cause." It was at last becoming obvious to everyone that the Federals had basically unlimited resources and manpower. It was simply inevitable that they would eventually win the war. By January 1, 1865, there were more than 620,000 troops serving in the Federal forces. By that time, there were less than 197,000 serving in the Confederate forces, and some were old men and young boys. The Confederate economy was in shambles, while the U.S. economy was booming greater than ever before with wartime production going full tilt. By May 1, 1865, there were more than one million men in the U.S. forces, while the Confederate forces had collapsed; the South's main armies had surrendered or were in the process of surrendering. General Lee had surrendered to General Grant on April 9, and General Johnston had surrendered to General Sherman on April 26. It was not until May 9 that Gen. Nathan Bedford Forrest surrendered his command, as part of Gen. Richard Taylor's forces; it was the last Confederate army to surrender east of the Mississippi. Forrest had been the quintessential Confederate cavalry officer. A rugged individual with an inborn sense of military strategy, he was combative, rebellious, fearsome, and charismatic. Wounded four times during the war, he had personally killed thirty Federal soldiers in hand-to-hand combat and had had a total of twenty-nine horses shot out from under him: "a horse ahead," as he described it. To many he was, and still is, the very incarnation of the Confederate Cause itself.

In Tennessee, the Federal military governor, Andrew Johnson, took steps to establish a civil government prior to his departure for inauguration as vice president of the United States on March 4. He arranged for a convention by the exec-utive committee of the National Union Party, a temporary fusion of the pro-Union elements of the Democratic and

Republican Parties. It was an informal sort of convention; no one was elected to it, and any professed Unionist could attend. This convention voted to annul the actions of the 1861 secessionist state legislature and ratified all the actions of the outgoing military government. It also assumed the powers of a nominating committee for candidates for state offices and drew up a single slate, on which the nominee for governor was William G. "Parson" Brownlow of Knoxville. As the only candidate, Brownlow was automatically elected. Thus, through the action of a minority of its voters, Tennessee began moving along a path which would make it the first former Confederate state to return to civil government with the United States.

All the cruel war's battles and skirmishes now passed onto the pages of history and began fading into the gunsmoke-clouded memories of old veterans. Thousands of those veterans told poignant tales of long marches and hard battles in Tennessee. With 1,462 armed clashes, the Volunteer State had the second largest number of military engagements during the war (only Virginia had more). Tennessee was also the scene of some of the war's largest and bloodiest battles. Today the beautiful hills and fields of Tennessee no longer echo with the sounds of battle. Few of its citizens would wish to return to such a hard and violent time. Yet anyone who is thrilled by tales of adventure cannot help but be fascinated by such a dangerous era in the state's history. The desperate conflict's dramatic record of personal bravery and self-sacrifice will always endure as a treasured portion of Tennessee's rich heritage.

Afterword:
Reconstruction in Tennessee

The end of the war in Tennessee brought bitterness, hatred, and vengeance rather than peace. The Reconstruction Era in the state was filled with turmoil and violence as the victorious Unionists, led by their fanatical governor, sought retribution on their fellow Tennesseans who had sided with the South.

Governor William G. Brownlow had come to office for the express purpose of punishing Confederate sympathizers and erasing from Tennessee all traces of their influence. In his younger years he had been a Methodist minister, riding circuits in Tennessee, Virginia, and North Carolina. But his true calling was politics. As editor of a Knoxville newspaper, Brownlow had expressed his Unionist, antislavery sentiments. When the war finally came, he spent time in jail for his outspoken nature. As the war came to an end with the Federals victorious, he made his move for the position of Unionist governor. Through masterful political maneuvering and intrigue, he succeeded in gaining office.

In June 1865, at Governor Brownlow's urging, the Tennessee legislature passed a franchise bill designed to ensure Unionist political dominance. Former Confederate military and civilian officials, men who had left Federal or state offices to serve the Confederate government, and those who had fled Union-occupied territory, were all denied the right to vote for the next fifteen years. All other former Confederates in Tennessee were disenfranchised for five years and could regain the right to vote only by taking an "iron-clad" loyalty oath and securing witnesses who would swear to their loyalty. In the spring of the following year, the state legislature passed an even more restrictive act which permanently disenfranchised all former Confederate supporters. The legislature also authorized Brownlow to appoint in each county special registrars to judge each voter's qualifications. To enforce these measures, Brownlow was granted the power to organize special militia companies to guard polling places against threats from the Ku Klux Klan, protect registrars, enforce franchise restrictions, and prevent interference with an election.

Vindictive acts such as those promoted by Brownlow had led to the formation of the Ku Klux Klan. The vigilante organization was founded in December 1865 in Pulaski, Tennessee, by a group of Confederate veterans, the best known of whom was none other than Nathan Bedford Forrest. Many white Southerners welcomed the arrival of the Klan as a force to defend them against the oppression of the radical Unionists.

The excesses of Governor Brownlow and his radical Unionists became increasingly unpopular, and former Confederates as well as conservative Unionists chipped away at the vindictive governor's power. Even with the franchise restrictions, Brownlow's administration grew gradually weaker as ex-Confederates and conservatives became increasingly stronger in the struggle for control of postwar Tennessee. Brownlow's egotism and vaulting ambition alienated many, including some of his strongest supporters. He nevertheless won a second term as governor in 1867. However, his attempts to win a broader base of support by winning over African-Americans to his vindictive cause failed. Brownlow realized his time was short, so he chose a U.S. Senate seat over the governorship in 1869. At last his tyrannical reign in Tennessee was over. His successor as governor, DeWitt Senter, disbanded the

hated state militia shortly after taking office. Eventually, he ended voting restrictions and completely dismantled Brownlow's programs.

The Ku Klux Klan's Grand Wizard, Nathan Bedford Forrest, sensed victory in Tennessee and also recognized that the Klan had gone the uncontrollable, lawless way of all vigilante organizations. Therefore, in 1869, he ordered it to disband. Of course, it never did dissolve but instead went on to create its own legacy of vengeance and violence. The Klan grew stronger with its members riding a bloody trail into and through the twentieth century and surviving even into the twenty-first as archaic ghosts in an outdated, reoccurring nightmare of the Reconstruction Era.

Bibliography

Alderson, William T. and Hulan Glyn Thomas. *Historic Sites in Tennessee*. Nashville: The Tennessee Historical Commission, 1963.

Barrow, Charles Kelly and J. H. Segars and R. B. Rosenburg, eds. *Forgotten Confederates: An Anthology about Black Southerners*. Atlanta, GA: Southern Heritage Press, 1995.

Bearss, Edwin C. "The Fall of Fort Henry Tennessee." Eastern National Park and Monument Association. Reprinted from *The West Tennessee Historical Society*, Vol. XVII, 1963.

Catton, Bruce. *The American Heritage Picture History of the Civil War*. New York: American Heritage/Bonanza Books, 1960.

Cornish, Dudley Taylor. *The Sable Arm: Black Troops in the Union Army, 1861-1865*. Lawrence, KS: University Press of Kansas, 1987.

Davis, William C. and Bell I. Wiley, eds. *The Civil War: the Compact Edition*. Vol. II. New York: Black Dog and Leventhal Publishers, 1994.

Dillahunty, Albert. *Shiloh*. Washington, D.C.: Government Printing Office, 1955.

Fisher, Noel C. *War at Every Door: Partisan Politics and Guerrilla Violence in East Tennessee, 1860-1869.* Chapel Hill, NC: The University of North Carolina Press, 1997.

Foote, Shelby. *The Civil War: A Narrative.* Volumes I-III. New York: Random House, 1974.

Gordon, D. T. Unpublished letter to James Gordon dated 1-16-65. Courtesy of Dale Gordon, great-grandson of D. T. Gordon.

Grant, Ulysses S. *Personal Memoirs of U. S. Grant.* Edited by E. B. Long. New York: Da Capo Press, 1982.

Hauptman, Laurence M. *Between Two Fires: American Indians in the Civil War.* New York: The Free Press, 1995.

Hughes, Benjamin F. "Diary of Benjamin F. Hughes 1835-1875." Unpublished memoirs. Courtesy of Irving Merry, great-grandson of Hughes.

Korn, Jerry and the Editors of Time-Life Books. *The Fight for Chattanooga.* Alexandria, VA: Time-Life Books Inc., 1985.

Korn, Jerry and the Editors of Time-Life Books. *War on the Mississippi.* Alexandria, VA: Time-Life Books Inc., 1985.

McPherson, James M. *Battle Cry of Freedom: The Civil War Era.* New York: Oxford University Press, 1988.

Miller, Francis Trevelyan, ed. *The Photographic History of the Civil War: The Opening Battles.* New York: Castle Books, 1957.

Nevin, David and the Editors of Time-Life Books. *The Road to Shiloh.* Alexandria, VA: Time-Life Books Inc., 1983.

Nevin, David and the Editors of Time-Life Books. *Sherman's March.* Alexandria, VA: Time-Life Books Inc., 1986.

Page, Dave. *Ships Versus Shore: Civil War Engagements along Southern Shores and Rivers.* Nashville, TN: Rutledge Hill Press, 1994.

Street, James, Jr. and the Editors of Time-Life Books. *The Struggle for Tennessee: Tupelo to Stones River.* Alexandria, VA: Time-Life Books Inc., 1985.

Sullivan, James R. *Chickamauga and Chattanooga Battlefields.* Washington, D.C.: Government Printing Office, 1956.

Watkins, Sam R. *Co. Aytch: A Side Show of the Big Show.* New York: Simon & Schuster Inc., 1990.

Index to Battles and Skirmishes

BATTLE	DATE	PAGE
Chickamauga (GA)	Sept. 19-20, 1863	92-94
Blue Springs	Oct. 10, 1863	108
Wauhatchie	Oct. 28, 1863	99-100
Orchard Knob (Chattanooga)	Nov. 23, 1863	100
Lookout Mountain (Chattanooga)	Nov. 24, 1863	100-101
Missionary Ridge (Chattanooga)	Nov. 25, 1863	101-6
Fort Sanders (Knoxville)	Nov. 28-29, 1863	108-10
Gatlinburg	Dec. 10, 1863	110
Fort Pillow	April 12, 1864	111-13
Brice's Crossroads (MS)	June 10, 1864	114
Tupelo (MS)	July 14, 1864	114
Greeneville	Sept. 4, 1864	117
Johnsonville	Nov. 4, 1864	118
Spring Hill	Nov. 29, 1864	119
Franklin	Nov. 30, 1864	119-25
Nashville	Dec. 15-16, 1864	124-29

About the Author

Steve Cottrell is a former high school teacher and a graduate of Missouri Southern State College and Pittsburg State University. He is the author of *Civil War in the Indian Territory* and *Civil War in Texas and New Mexico Territory* as well as coauthor of *Civil War in the Ozarks,* also published by Pelican. Steve's great-great-grandfather, John P. Cottrell, served in the Civil War in Tennessee as a private in the Sixth Indiana Cavalry Regiment. John's record states that he participated in the East Tennessee Campaign and the Siege of Nashville.

About the Artist

In addition to his regular artwork, artist Andy Thomas has been documenting the Trans-Mississippi battles of the Civil War. He has also illustrated and provided cover art for many books, including *Civil War in the Ozarks, Civil War in Texas and New Mexico Territory,* and *Civil War in the Indian Territory.* He works out of Maze Creek Studio in Carthage, Missouri—www.andythomas.com or 1-800-432-1581.